Creating the
ART of the GAME

Matthew Omernick

New Riders

1249 Eighth Street, Berkeley, California 94710

An Imprint of Peachpit, A Division of Pearson Education

CREATING THE ART OF THE GAME

International Standard Book Number: 0-7357-1409-6

Library of Congress Catalog Card Number: 2003116669

Printed in the United States of America

First printing: March, 2004

06   7 6 5 4 3

TRADEMARKS

WARNING AND DISCLAIMER

Publisher
Stephanie Wall

Production Manager
Gina Kanouse

Senior Acquisitions Editor
Linda Bump Harrison

Development Editor
Chris Zahn

Project Editor
Michael Thurston

Copy Editor
Toni Ackley

Senior Indexer
Cheryl Lenser

Proofreader
Beth Trudell

Composition
ContentWorks

Manufacturing Coordinator
Dan Uhrig

Interior Designer
Kim Scott

Cover Designer
Aren Howell

Marketing
Scott Cowlin
Tammy Detrich

Publicity Manager
Susan Nixon

CONTENTS AT A GLANCE

Table of Contents

DEDICATION

This book is dedicated to my wonderful family
who has always encouraged and supported me.

ABOUT THE AUTHOR

Matthew Omernick currently works as a lead artist for LucasArts Entertainment Company near San Francisco, CA. With a B.F.A. from The Ringling School of Art and Design in Sarasota, FL, Matt has more than seven years of industry experience as a 3D artist and animator.

Matt has also taught college-level 3D graphics for four years at Cal State Fullerton and the Academy of Art College in downtown San Francisco. He has worked for companies such as DreamWorks, Day 1 Studios, and Electronic Arts. He began his career working for various film and broadcast studios in Florida and Chicago, then branched into creating 3D art for video games. Some of Matt's credited titles include the *Medal of Honor*™ series, *RTX Red Rock*, and *Secret Weapons Over Normandy*. He is currently working on several cutting edge projects for multiple platforms.

ABOUT THE TECHNICAL REVIEWERS

These reviewers contributed their considerable hands-on expertise to the entire development process for *Creating the Art of the Game*. As the book was being written, these dedicated professionals reviewed all the material for technical content, organization, and flow. Their feedback was critical to ensuring that *Creating the Art of the Game* fits our readers' need for the highest-quality technical information.

Danny Oros, deeply inspired by graphic computer games from the Commodore 64 and early PCs era, is a self-taught 2D and 3D computer game artist with a hobbyist background in games programming. First employed as a computer artist at Ubisoft in the late 1990s, he then moved on to become the Lead Technical Artist at Matrox Graphics. There, he contributed greatly to the direction and development of technologically advanced graphics demonstrations, raising eyebrows at such events as SIGGRAPH.

Danny continues to explore and exploit the art of technology as Technical Director on game projects at Ubisoft, Montreal, Canada.

Jay Faircloth has been a freelance illustrator and designer for the better part of the last 15 years. In the last four years his focus has shifted from traditional media to digital art, and he has contributed artwork and textures to several popular fan-created "mods," most notably *Marathon: Resurrection* for *Unreal Tournament*. He currently works as a Project Manager at Harvard University, but would gladly throw it all away for a career in the game business.

ACKNOWLEDGMENTS

Listed below are just some of the amazing people I'd like to thank!

Peter Hirschmann—For his support, encouragement, and amazingly written foreword.

Linda Harrison—For her patience, assistance, and knowledge.

Chris Zahn—Without Chris's hard work and organizational skills, you would not be reading this book today.

Mark Barbolak, Tom Sarris, and John Garrett—The diligent and enthusiastic attorneys who helped make this all possible.

Steve Groll—For his pivotal role in the permissions game.

Molly Mendoza—One of the greatest artists I know. Thanks for contributing!

Paul Murphy—Paul's knowledge and artist skills helped give this book its depth and value.

Ian Berry—For his talent and artistic offerings.

Dmitri Ellingson—Much thanks to D, my mentor and great friend.

Eric Burke—A more supportive and creative friend than anyone could ask for.

Robin Roepstorff—The Deutschlander with all the answers.

Terry Roepstorff—An inspiration to me, and everyone who knows her.

Peter Choe—100% artist, 100% friend.

Matt White—For his excitement and encouragement.

Heather Kobrin—Without Heather's design skills, the vision for this book would have not seen the light of day.

Lynne Gura—The enthusiastic and genuine artist who kept me going.

Paul Edmonson—What happens when a right-brained artist like myself needs left brain answers?

Gary Omernick—My loving father who continues to serve as an inspiration to everyone he knows.

Linda Myers—My loving mother whose support and respect means the world to me.

Glen Myers—Her caring husband and my stepfather.

Meghan Omernick—The greatest sister one could ever ask for. And one of my best friends.

Cassia Dominguez—Graphic designer extraordinaire.

Jon Slusser—His confidence in me launched my teaching career.

And to all the game developers who have invested their passion and life-blood into entertaining us all.

TELL US WHAT YOU THINK

As the reader of this book, you are the most important critic and commentator. We value your opinion and want to know what we're doing right, what we could do better, what areas you'd like to see us publish in, and any other words of wisdom you're willing to pass our way.

When you contact us, please be sure to include this book's title, ISBN, and author, as well as your name and email address. We will carefully review your comments and share them with the author and editors who worked on the book.

Email: errata@peachpit.com

Making Games

Congratulations! You have made a most excellent career choice. Other than official ice cream taster or full-time massage school test subject, there aren't many jobs better than this one. I would even argue that making entertainment is a noble calling, because if done right, it can make people happy. And that's not bad for a day's work.

But this is not a career for the faint of heart. One of the things that can make our industry so exciting is also one of things that makes it so difficult: *rapid evolution*. New platforms, new versions, new techniques—things are always emerging from the ether that force you to adapt and grow. You will be hard-pressed to find another industry where *how* you do something can change so radically from year to year.

That's why it is so important to develop a core understanding of *why* things work the way they do. The big book you now hold in your hands will help you evolve and adapt in the world of making games. It will give you that core understanding of game art fundamentals that will make you successful now and, more importantly, in the future.

Matt Omernick is one of the most talented artists I've ever worked with, and I can't think of a better person to share with you his knowledge and experience.

TURNING LEAD INTO GOLD, PLASTIC, WOOD, ETC.

A good game artist is a modern-day alchemist, conjuring up not just mere objects from polygons and pixels, but entire worlds. Imagine this tome is really an illuminated manuscript, forged on ancient parchment by the flicker of candlelight, revealing all the mystical secrets of creation.[1] The centuries-old goal of transforming lead into gold is now a reality—achieved through the simple changing of a texture.

Whatever the medium—poetry, painting, sculpture, photographry—the job of an artist is often to interpret the world. This has never been more literal than with a game artist, someone who is using a toolset that was, a few decades ago, not just unknown but inconceivable. Never forget, though, that a quality toolset can empower a good artist, but it doesn't make you one. Only passion and talent can do that.

Like Matt, the best artists I know are the ones who have a love of the world around them. They're always seeking out new adventures and experiences, moving and traveling—always searching for more data on how the world works. (And they never go anywhere without their digital camera, because you never know when a texture reference will present itself.)

How does water splash? How does smoke billow? How does metal rust? How do buildings crumble? How the world is put together is the key to understanding how to interpret it. Knowing the way pieces fit together is crucial for building up a game world, but let's face it, most games deal with blowing stuff up in one form or another—so knowing how to successfully deconstruct an environment is also a key skill to have.

EMBRACE THE CONSTRAINTS

In the year 2098, Amalgamated Global Electronic Entertainment Inc. will release their highly anticipated FunStation 3000 game console. It will feature 14 million terabytes of RAM, a quantum-holographic optical drive of near-infinite storage capacity, and will have multiprocessor performance that exceeds the speed of light. I guarantee you game developers will still complain it's not powerful enough.

---

[1] Actually, I'm pretty sure Matt wrote this on his computer. The only candles involved would have come from him having a girl over for dinner.

Making games is all about being creative inside the confines of the technology. This applies to all disciplines—engineering, design, sound—but often has the biggest impact on you, the artist. The best artists determine their boundaries as quickly as possible and then get busy. You will be a much happier person once you accept that you will never, ever have as much power or memory as you want.

A few more points of unsolicited advice:

- Play games—This seems like a no-brainer, but you'd be surprised by how many people who work in the industry don't play games. Actually, it's an easy trap to fall into when you're in crunch mode trying to meet deadlines. Anything that doesn't involve eating or sleeping starts to fall off the priority list, but be careful—looking at competitive products and seeing how other people solved their problems can be very helpful. Besides, how can you make a fun game if you're not making time to have fun yourself?

- Engineers are your friends—They usually have the hardest jobs on the project, so be nice to them. Bring them soda and candy on a daily basis. An engineer that gets passionate about art tech can do wonders for you.

- Learn to communicate with nonartists—In addition to the engineers, it takes a large group of people with an incredibly diverse skill set to create a game. Every job on a team is intertwined, so make an effort to understand everyone's role. A beautiful outdoor environment can be ruined if the ambient audio sucks.

- Steal from the real world—One of my favorite tenets of game design (no matter the genre) is that the real world is always more interesting than anything we can make up. The same rule can be applied to art as well. The classic LucasArts game *Dark Forces II: Jedi Knight* is a prime example of this. Even though it was set in the fantasy world of *Star Wars*, the environments still made real-world sense. Inside a spaceport you could find an extremely logical architectural progression: from the entertainment area for pilots and crew to cluttered maintenance bays, then onto giant refueling pipes that led underneath the docking area, then up to the massive ships themselves. The whole thing was filthy. And it felt real.

- Hone your traditional skills—Never lose sight that you are an artist first, game artist second. Continue to take figure drawing classes, photograph for pleasure, sculpt on weekends—whatever floats your boat. The work you do outside of games will inform the work you do inside.

The best advice I can give you, though, is don't wait around for people to give you advice. Creating art is something you only learn by doing, and reading this book will help you on your way. You're already one step ahead of the game.

—Peter Hirschmann, writer and producer of *Medal of Honor*™

[INTRODUCTION]

WELCOME TO THE WONDERFUL WORLD of video game art. Creating 3D art for games is one of the most challenging, exciting, and rewarding paths one can pursue. Think about it: Having the opportunity to create entire worlds, interesting characters, and new adventures, and then bringing them all together into a piece of entertainment has to be one of the most satisfying experiences one can have as an artist. The skills and experience you can gain working in games will make you a valuable asset to any part of the computer graphics industry. With the line between prerendered CG and real-time 3D blurring more and more every day, this book is meant to give you a unique perspective along with the foundational skills you'll need for a successful career as a 3D game artist.

The following chapters will take you from start to finish through the process and responsibilities of making a video game from an artist's point of view. At the same time, I'll be offering scores of effective tips and tricks used by some of the most successful game artists in the industry today. Whether you are already a seasoned 3D artist or are working your way into the industry, I hope you'll find the information in this book to be straightforward and valuable.

WHO SHOULD READ THIS BOOK?

I am assuming that you have an art background and have had at least some experience with a 3D software package, whether it be Maya, 3ds max, LightWave, or any other 3D program available on the market today. I've done my best to ensure that the contents and lessons presented in this book do not focus on one piece of software, and are applicable no matter what program you might use. In cases where it is essential to point out specific features or functions, I've chosen to highlight Maya and 3ds max as examples because I feel they represent the most common and understandable characteristics of 3D software used in developing today's games.

In addition to having some 3D experience, I'm also assuming that you have some knowledge of digital painting and image editing software, such as Photoshop or Painter. All of the image editing in this book will focus on Photoshop. Not only is Photoshop the most frequently used package in the industry, but its long history and usability have made it the core example for most computer graphics programs available today.

But of all the skills and experience I could hope you have, creativity will be the most valuable.

A TRUE ARTIST FIRST

The most important advice I can offer you, and a recurring theme in this book, is that in order to be a successful game artist, you need to focus on your traditional art skills.

What does it mean to be an artist? It means thinking creatively. Artists have a certain sense of design and aesthetics; they can draw, paint, sing, or dance. But what really sets us apart is our ability to imagine and create. Whether you were born with a creative predisposition, or you've trained your mind and skills over the years, the outcome is the same. It's the way we see and feel the world around us that makes us unique and valuable. Unfortunately, many people that pursue 3D art do not realize the value of true artistic skills…and it shows.

You can spend all your time learning the ins and outs of the latest software, playing the latest games, and working though every tutorial you can find, but that will not make you a good artist. Software upgrades and games transform, but the one thing that never changes is the artist inside you. That is why it is so important to focus and develop your traditional art skills in order to keep yourself valuable and happy now and in the future. Using and developing your artistic eye is also what will set you apart from the amateurs.

The bottom line is, it doesn't matter whether we are using a computer, a paintbrush, a pencil, charcoal, or clay. What makes us unique is our artistic core.

WHAT TO EXPECT FROM THIS BOOK

The value of this book is intended to be in the presentation of the material. I've done my best to propose the ideas in a manner that is clear, concise, exciting, and most importantly, retainable. I attribute my success as a teacher and art director to these same principles.

Although I went to a very good school, I found that quite frequently, many of my instructors would ask us to read and work through a basic tutorial from the software's manual for that day's assignment. I quickly realized I didn't need to pay college tuition to read a manual. I wanted real-world perspectives and experiences. Because of this, I am avoiding the approach and structure of a manual at all costs. Instead, I try to create an enjoyable, exciting experience that takes you through, step by step, what it is like to be a game artist while offering the experiences and methods I have learned in over six years in the industry.

You will notice that there are a couple of topics that are not covered in this book. I do not focus on animation or character modeling because although these are both obviously parts of game art, animation is, of course, an art form in itself, and it requires a very different approach and workflow than modeling, texturing, and lighting. Discussing animation would be another book entirely! So, I've chosen to focus on the idea of building and populating worlds, which I feel is the most broad, yet clear, way to put forth the ideas and techniques. The related subject of character modeling and texturing is also only touched upon lightly in the hopes that many of the offered ideas are equally applicable to creating characters.

WHAT THIS BOOK COVERS

Chapter 1, "Preparing to Create," delves into the use of reference as a source of inspiration and direction for your art.

Chapter 2, "Modeling Theory," provides the theories and common practices of polygonal modeling and how it fits into the big picture of production.

Chapter 3, "Introduction to Texturing," discusses the essential information you need to know to create textures for use in a game.

Chapter 4, "Advanced Texturing," explores methods and examples that help you create textures of the highest quality.

Chapter 5, "Applying Textures," offers lessons and information on UV mapping and editing, teaching you how to wrap your textures onto your models.

Chapter 6, "Advanced Modeling," takes polygonal modeling to the next level while discussing alternate modeling methods and geometry types.

Chapter 7, "Lighting Principles," discusses lighting theory and practices used not only for games, but also various mediums such as photography and film.

Chapter 8, "In-Game Lighting," takes the theories of traditional lighting and offers lessons on how to apply them to video games. Topics include vertex lighting, lightmaps, and other lighting methods.

Chapter 9, "Effects," breaks down the process and explains how special effects are generated for games. It discusses everything from particle effects to creating fog and other atmospherics.

Chapter 10, "Tips and Tricks," touches on many of the creative solutions that are used by game artists to make the best-looking art possible.

Chapter 11, "User Interface Design and Creation," talks about the theories and responsibilities of an artist tasked with creating the user interface for games.

Chapter 12, "Wrapping It Up," brings all the methods and lessons into perspective by looking at how a game comes together in the end. You'll learn about the final touches such as collision geometry, bug fixing, and artistic polish.

Download all accompanying files at http://www.peachpit.com/title/0735714096?redir=1.

MAKING THE GAME

For those of you who can remember the days before video games became commonplace, most kids were playing board games like Battleship, Mousetrap, or Checkers. Soon, there was quite a new option available to us: a game you could actually play on your TV. It would actually react to your commands! Our imaginations stretched: "Wow, I am a Pong paddle!" "I have the skill to jump across an alligator!"

"I rule the world!" That is what attracts us to video games: having the capability to transport ourselves into new and unusual situations…and conquer them. There is nothing more satisfying than saving the princess or defeating the alien invaders. Games are about fun.

The same is true today. You can create the greatest game art in the world, but if the game isn't fun, the game won't sell, and your beautiful artwork will not be seen! For this reason, it is in your best interest to get as involved as possible with the entire process of game development. Take responsibility for the game and do whatever you can to motivate and inspire the rest of your team. Making a personal investment in your game and your team can make all the difference in the world.

The process of making a video game is much more complex than most people imagine. To someone who has never been involved in the production of a video game, it may seem quite simple. You come up with a good idea, hire some people, and get to work until you are done, right? Of course, it's not quite that easy. There are always unforeseen issues, missed deadlines, seemingly impossible hurdles, and many long hours. As you read through this book, I think you'll see how involved and complex the responsibilities of a game artist can be, and realize that making a video game is no simple task. You'll also find that the challenges you'll face will equal the sense of achievement and glory you'll feel when it is all said and done.

Games are naturally becoming more focused and refined with near photo-realistic environments and characters, precise gameplay, and entertaining stories. There is an indisputable trend that the concept of what is a video game is changing rapidly. So, it's extremely important for you to keep your finger on the pulse of the industry and make yourself as knowledgeable as possible about games of all types.

As an example, a massively multiplayer online role-playing game (MMORPG) is quite different from a single player first person shooter (FPS). It used to be that games were games, and as a gamer, you got your hands on everything you could. But in recent years, games have found their niche crowds and target audiences. Someone who enjoys action adventure games or puzzle games may have no interest in role-playing games (RPGs). Someone who enjoys RPGs may not care about strategy games. With the industry growing so rapidly and the popularity of games increasing exponentially, there is room for all types of games and all types of gamers. Virtual reality is already in our face. As a game artist (or real-time entertainment artist), you have the opportunity to define and mold this emerging medium. It's a very exciting time to get involved in games.

Before we move on to Chapter 1, I think it's important for us to compare the different platforms for which games can be created. For simplicity's sake, I'll divide platforms into two categories: PC games and console games. PC games, of course, refer to games that are designed for and played on your home computer. Console games are games that run on systems like PlayStation 2, Xbox, and GameCube. Developing games for each platform is quite different, and each has its advantages and disadvantages.

PC games are typically easier to program for and allow the artist larger texture resolutions. On the other hand, developing a game for PC means that you have to take into account the variety of computer systems that the game needs to run on. Some people may have extremely fast gaming machines capable of rendering a staggering amount of information. However, your game also has to be able to run on a slower PC with less memory. You try to cater to your core audience and make assumptions on the speed of their machines, but you still have to develop the game with the lowest common denominator in mind.

With consoles, we know that everyone has the exact same hardware, so you can push the limits without worrying about little Jimmy and his PII 300MHz machine. From a programming standpoint, Xbox is easier to program for than the PS2 because it is essentially a PC in a black box. Xbox also provides developers with an internal hard drive that can be used to save game levels or content and saves time loading from a disk.

As an artist, it's important to be able to continually adjust depending on the type of game you are working on and the type of platform on which it will be played. Your job is to be an artist first and foremost, and your greatest skill and advantage will be creative problem solving. Be confident and be invested in what you do. But also be flexible so that you can produce art that is efficient as well as high in quality.

THEMES

As you move through the material in this book, you'll find many recurring themes. In fact, I'm sure you'll hear them so often it'll drive you crazy. But trust me, it's for your own good! Hopefully, along with the lessons and explanations, these repetitive themes will stay with you and change the way you look at art in general.

Just remember to think for yourself, open your mind, and most importantly, have a great time. So let's get to it!

[**CHAPTER**]   1

PREPARING TO CREATE

USING REFERENCE PLAYS AN ESSENTIAL ROLE in the process of creating a quality game. Gathering and studying reference can make the difference between an exceptional game and a mediocre product.

Here is a perfect example. Let's say you want to draw a portrait of a friend. You could sit down, imagine what he or she looks like, and start to draw. However, you'll get a very different result than if you had used a photo or had that person in front of you. With a reference, you'll be able to capture the subtleties and details you would never be able to think of on your own. Whether it's a person or a building, a reference gives you goals, direction, clues, and motivation.

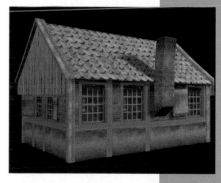

I know that we as artists sometimes think that looking at a reference is like cheating. We want to feel that we have the ability to create anything directly from our minds. And of course, a defining trait of artists is an active and creative imagination. But choosing the right reference is as artistic a skill as drawing itself. I cannot stress enough how critical reference can be to the outcome of your work.

How and Where to Collect Reference

As I mentioned, reference can be the key to realistic and beautiful artwork. But where is the best place to find it? Endless sources are available for gathering the information you need. You just have to know where and how to look.

I typically start by using search engines like Google.com that allow me to search images only. But be creative in your search. If you are modeling a comfortable couch, for example, don't just see what comes up for the word "couch"; expand your search for lounge chairs, or La-Z-Boy, or even cushions. You may find a detail or feature that makes your couch that much more interesting and unique. When you are modeling or texturing, always stop and ask yourself if there is some detail you might be missing, and if you could find it online. Take the extra two minutes to search for a photo of the object or texture you are working on. I think you'll be surprised at how many details and ideas you'll get out of that two-minute investment.

While working on *Medal of Honor Frontline*™, I began creating the interior of a German U-boat submarine (see Figure 1.1). I first scoured the Internet to find any images of a German U-boat, inside or out. Next I searched for images of any kind of a submarine, it didn't have to be German, or even from WWII. Then I hit the books. I looked through any WWII book I could find, and scanned images of submarines. Next, I looked at the movies *Das Boot* and *U-571*, and I actually took the time to take screen captures of the scenes in the film that were useful to me. By this time I had gathered a good amount of quality reference material. But that was not enough.

I was sent to Chicago for the only remaining WWII-era German U-boat tour in the United States. This is where my reference hunting paid off. Being able not only to photograph anything I wanted, but also to touch, smell, hear, and experience what it was like to be crammed into this unique and claustrophobic atmosphere truly changed the way I approached the creation of that particular level in the game. There were so many ideas and details that I found on that tour that it drastically changed my direction and standard. As a nice side effect, this information motivated me to do something special and gave me the opportunity to establish a level of detail I know had not been achieved before. The bottom line is, you can never have too much reference material as an artist.

1.1 A screenshot of the German U-boat in *Medal of Honor Frontline*™.

SEEK THE BEST

If you are fortunate enough to work for a company that is willing to go the extra mile to make a project great, you can hope to travel and seek out the best reference possible. For *Medal of Honor Frontline*™, the art and sound teams took several trips, including a two-week romp through Germany, Holland (see Figure 1.2), and France to take digital photos of buildings, signs, and other objects. Figure 1.3 provides a look at the 3D representation that grew out of the photo shown in Figure 1.2.

1.2 A reference photo taken in Holland.

1.3 The 3D interpretation. The photo was used more for details and ideas rather than exact re-creation.

Medal of Honor Frontline™ IMAGES COURTESY OF ELECTRONIC ARTS INC. © 2002 ELECTRONIC ARTS INC. ALL RIGHTS RESERVED.

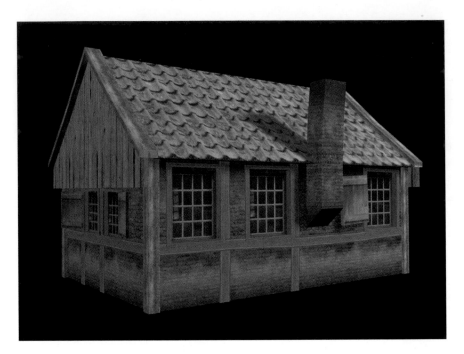

CONCEPT ART

On most teams, you'll find at least one or more concept artists whose job is to previsualize and create art for use as reference, color compositions, and just good old-fashioned inspiration. Concept art is vital to a production for numerous reasons. Establishing the look and feel of the game before production even starts makes for a more solid concept and is conducive to a quality final product. Even though your company may have dedicated concept artists, don't use that as an excuse to quit drawing! Keep in mind that even if you are a modeler, a texture artist, or a character animator, you should always be your own concept artist. Previsualizing the images you have in your head before you start to work on the computer is always a good idea. It keeps that traditional artist inside you alive! Keep in mind that the computer is just another tool. Continuing to develop your drawing skills will significantly improve the rest of your work and increase your value as an artist. Figure drawing is one of the best exercises for practicing and refining your understanding of shape and line. It also makes for a strong (and many times required) addition to your portfolio.

Using concept art to establish the look and feel of your game before you jump into producing assets creates a clear sense of direction and saves time and money. A good concept artist will choose compositions that reveal as much information about the scene, character, or object as possible. Figure 1.4 presents a solid example of concept art.

1.4 Concept art from LucasArts' *Gladius*. The drawing presents us with mood, lighting, texture, space, and detail. The more information a piece of concept art can provide, the better. Did you notice the human figures in the trees?

Concept art can also help to foreshadow issues that may come up in production. For example, let's say you draw out a character you imagine to be in the game. He looks super-cool and is exciting to imagine in action. But as you start to imagine how this character will be built, rigged, animated, and so on, you may come across some potential issues. Maybe the cost of creating a realistic cloth simulation for the cape is too much. Maybe the gear around his belt will interfere with a common movement he will perform. So just by creating a concept of the character first, you may be able to avoid some technical pitfalls that would cost the production a lot of time and money. This is where collaboration between the concept artist, modelers, and animators becomes all-important. Keeping an open and collaborative dialogue between the members of your team makes for a mutually respectful and efficient workflow.

Another advantage to relying on traditional drawing is that you can quickly think through a complex object and how it functions without spending the time to build it in 3D. You may be the fastest modeler on the planet, but concept artists are trained to quickly visualize and experiment with the ideas presented to them. Being able to test theory before production starts gives you a logical and precise advantage. Many concept artists are skilled in premodeling complicated objects to test their viability. Check out the concept art in Figure 1.5, which illustrates this point.

1.5 A previsualization of E. Z. Wheeler's mechanical arm from LucasArt's *RTX Red Rock*.

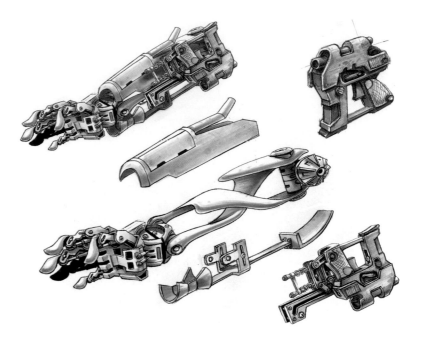

The most valuable application of concept art is that you have the opportunity to establish the overall look and feel of the game. Drawings of the environments, characters, color, and lighting studies all help the team envision the direction and visual fidelity of the game before anything is actually built. Just like a storyboard for a feature film, creating concept art and gathering reference play a very important part in defining what the game will be. Figures 1.6 and 1.7 represent this important aspect of concept art.

1.6 An environment concept from *Gladius*.

1.7 The 3D interpretation of the environment in the game.

Setting the Quality Bar

One distinct quality of an artist's personality is the need to continually improve on their own work. Embracing that desire in order to advance your skills and create better art can lead you to a successful and fulfilling career. The video game industry is one of the most technologically advanced industries in the world. The competition to outdo each other is what is driving programmers and artists to create newer, more realistic and challenging games. The research and development of artificial intelligence (AI) has made some of its most impressive leaps and bounds within the game industry. Creating a nonplayer character (NPC) that behaves and reacts like a real human being is a constant challenge, and a goal of game programmers and artists.

As an artist, some of the best homework you can do is to look at other games, movies, and artwork for inspiration and to see what others have done so you can take it one step further. Every time a new game or console is released, the expectation of the consumer is raised. It is our responsibility to improve and impress with each new project. And that is actually a big part of the fun. As you work, develop an attitude and ethic that drives you to improve on not only your own work, but also that of your peers. Staying on the cutting edge is a satisfying and rewarding endeavor. Looking at what has been done in the past and taking it to the next level is easy if you have the right attitude and passion.

BLOCKING OUT YOUR SCENE

Establishing a reliable and efficient workflow is essential to the development process. I constantly preach to my students and artists about using broad strokes to define your canvas and adding detail in layers. This method of working is easily comparable to painting an acrylic landscape (you know, with an actual paintbrush and real paint!). Let's say you are painting a mountain lake scene. You'd start with a large brush and a bluish color for the sky, covering the majority of the canvas. Next you'd add a layer of darker color to establish the horizon between the land and the sky. After that, maybe using a slightly smaller brush, you'd put in some rough mountains, then the lake, trees, clouds, and so on. You would continue to add details with more specific colors and smaller brushes until you have a finished product.

Now imagine painting the same landscape by starting in the upper left-hand corner, painting all the details, and then working your way across the canvas in the same manner. You'd go crazy, and the whole painting would be skewed. The same is true when creating something in 3D. You should always work in broad strokes. Add details and focus on one element at a time.

Another good example of this method is animating a character. In a walk cycle, you start by setting just two keyframes, one at point A and another at point B, moving the character across the screen from one place to another. Next, you would add keyframes for the up and down motion, then the legs, arms, head, and so on, until you have a polished and smooth walk.

Blocking out your scene is the first step to take in this process. Just like laying down that first layer of paint, we use simple primitive shapes to define scale and layout. Let's say we are building a small village. I always

> **NOTE**
>
> When working on a production, try to find out from the designers or character artists exactly how tall the characters in the game will be, and create a stand-in model that is a good average height. Also, make sure that the whole team has agreed on what units you'll be working with throughout the game, whether it be meters or feet and inches.

start my scene by importing a 5'11" character to use for scale. There doesn't need to be much detail to him, just a general shape that we can use to decide how tall a building is, or how wide a door should be (see Figure 1.8).

Next, create a large plane to act as the ground. When working in pre-production, the game designer and artist work together to create a very simple (sometimes crudely drawn) overhead map of how the environment might be laid out from a gameplay point of view (see Figure 1.9).

I typically scan and import this overhead map into the top view of my 3D viewport (see Figure 1.10). It's important for both the artist and the designer to work closely together to make sure you are both on the same page and to discuss each other's intentions.

Using the overhead map as a guide, create some simple primitives to act as placeholders for buildings, cars, trees, and the like (see Figure 1.11). This is a great starting point, and can immediately give you and the designer a sense of scale.

The next step is to get into the scene and, using your 5'11" character as reference, scale the objects as accurately as you can. In a very short period of time, you'll have a very basic, yet functional, scene that sets the size and scale of your project (see Figure 1.12). Broad stroke number 1!

1.8 A 5'11" stand-in character used for scale reference.

1.9 A simple overhead map to establish scale and layout.

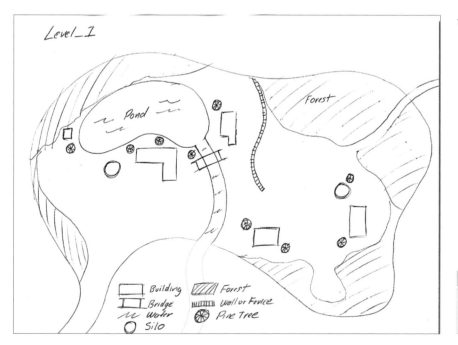

Level_1

Pond

Forest

Building

Bridge

Water

Silo

Forest

Wall or Fence

Pine Tree

NOTE

In 3ds max, go to the Views menu and choose Viewport Background.

1.10 The map imported into the Top view-port in Maya using an Image Plane.

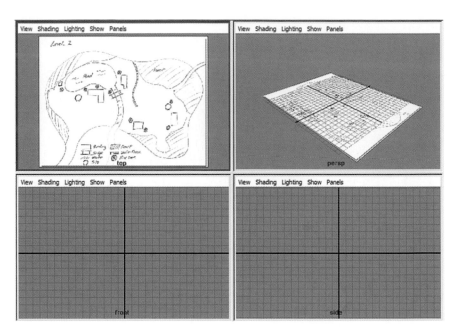

1.11 Using simple primitives to block out the major elements in a scene.

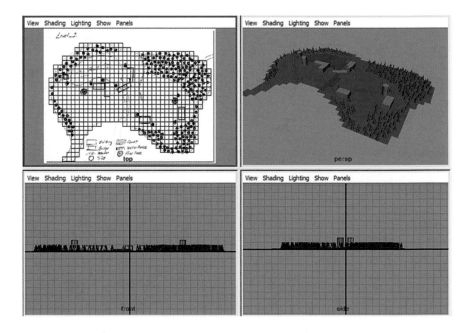

View Shading Lighting Show Panels

1.12 A blocked-out scene and a great start.

Another benefit to doing this, assuming your game engine is already working at this point, is that you can now export this simple scene into the game and actually run around as a player and verify that this is what you and the designer are looking for. (Some productions actually have the designer do this initial blocking out of a level, assuming they have some simple knowledge of 3D. I think it is important for both the artist and the level designer to have input at this point.)

Blocking out your scene isn't limited to modeling. This is also a great opportunity to throw in some simple lighting. Look at the concept art and color studies for that level. Toss in a few lights to establish a general feel and source, and verify that the angles and colors work in your scene. This can be as simple as adding one directional light and one ambient, tweaking the color and intensity a bit, and viewing the result. Now you have a great start and a lot to work with while knowing that your scale and proportions are nailed down. It's also a good idea to add a few simple textures at this point to remind yourself and others what types of materials these objects represent. Sometimes it can be as simple as writing the word "brick" on a texture and assigning it to anything you think may be brick. I usually grab some quick textures I already have that represent the materials that may be in the scene. You don't have to get too detailed yet, but maybe just introduce something that differentiates between grass and concrete, or brick and wood. Quite quickly, you will have a blocked-out scene that will improve and expedite the world-building process.

Conclusion

Starting a project on the right foot by collecting quality reference, conceptualizing your work, and setting a high standard for yourself will enable you to work efficiently and with focus. Get into the habit of working in broad strokes. Establish a canvas, and add detail as you progress. A successful preproduction process will get the ball rolling in the right direction.

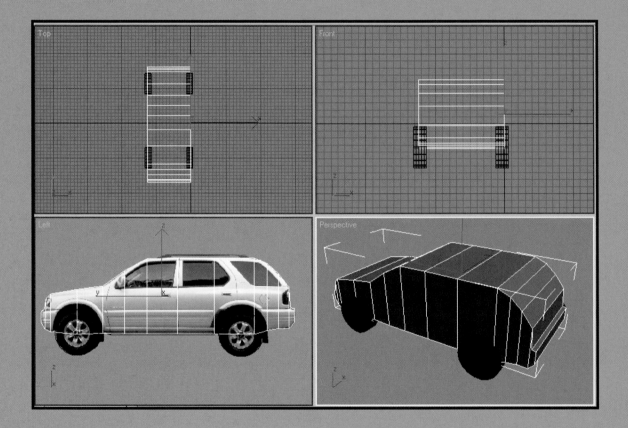

2

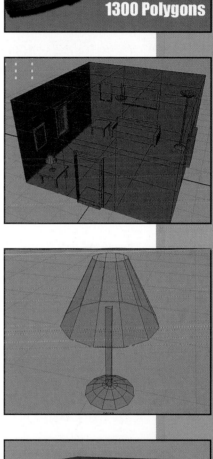

1300 Polygons

MODELING THEORY

THE PURPOSE OF THIS CHAPTER is to get into the proper frame of mind needed to understand the core philosophy of polygonal modeling for games. Understanding efficiency and the need for it when modeling is essential to creating game assets. Whether you are an experienced game artist or someone just learning the ropes, this chapter can provide the basic ideas and fundamental perspective that can make your experience as a modeler a fun and successful one.

Geometry types and modeling methods are as varied as drawing styles: NURBS, subdivision surfaces, patches, polygons—all have their advantages and serve many specific purposes. You'll find that although modeling for games requires a bit more thought and precision, the ability to create clean and efficient models is valuable in any 3D scenario. It's important to remember that no matter what method you use or how you go about building your objects and characters, it's the final product that counts. The practice of blocking out your models using broad strokes is particularly important when building solid and efficient geometry for use in an engine.

Despite the fact that there is no absolute "right" way to model for games, the process that you take in creating your geometry will play a very important role in how your final model looks and functions in a game environment. First off, being able to model quickly and efficiently is extremely valuable. Imagine you have only one month to work on a specific task; the faster you model and the fewer wasted polygons, the more time and raw materials you'll have to

work with. Hence, you should end up with a better-looking and more detailed product. On the other hand, maybe you can model extremely quickly, but are a bit sloppy, and you end up with stray vertices, overlapping faces, and T-junctions. This will catch up to you in the end when you have to go back to the model and spend the extra time to clean it up. We'll discuss some general rules you can follow to ensure you have stable and game-friendly geometry.

In this chapter I'll offer you some of the tools and methods I have found to be the most common and effective for 3D game modeling. For those of you who are new to 3D software and polygons, I'll outline some of the basics in the next section.

PRIMITIVES

Primitives are the simple shapes used as building blocks when modeling. Most 3D software programs offer the same primitive shapes. The most commonly used primitives are shown in Figure 2.1.

2.1 The same basic primitive shapes can be found in any polygonal modeling software.

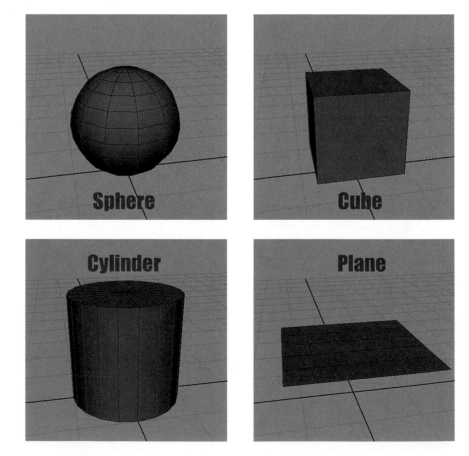

Primitives are a great starting point for almost any model because they enable you to start with broad strokes and add details as you go along. Think about drawing; any drawing instructor will teach you that you need to concentrate on the simple shapes that you see within an object. This helps define the dimensionality of a shape and maintains proportion. It also makes it easier for the artist to visualize the object as a collection of shapes that make up the whole. Take a look at Figure 2.2. The human body can be seen as being made up of simple primitive shapes.

The same is true for 3D modeling. Starting your model with primitives is also advantageous because you are starting with a clean, structured object, and building from that gives you a more reliable and solid framework with which to build your model. As you begin to model with this in mind, you'll find you start to see the world around you in a more clear and intuitive way.

2.2 Imagine the world around you as made up of simple primitive shapes.

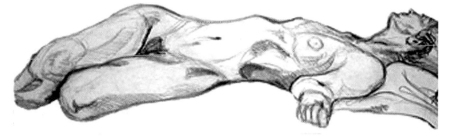

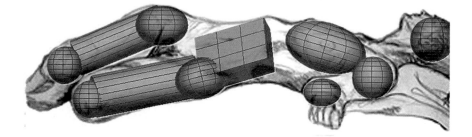

COMPONENTS

Components are the parts that make up a basic primitive or shape. You'll find they are very similar across all 3D packages. Once you create a primitive, you can of course scale it, move it, or rotate it. But when you want to alter or drastically change the shape, you go to the next level of control or detail, that of components. Vertices, edges, triangles (tris for short), faces, or elements—these are all different parts of the model that you can select and manipulate, giving you total control over the geometry. Not only can you do everything to a component that you can to a primitive, like scale, move, and rotate, but you also can extrude, merge, divide, or even texture on a component basis. See Figure 2.3 for a few examples of component types.

Terminology varies slightly among software packages. For example, in 3ds max a tri is called a face, and a face is called a polygon. But don't let it confuse you; all the same elements are there, some just happen to be named differently. The term *polygon* actually means "many sided," so, again, the terminology differs among packages. Just remember that a polygon can mean one or more triangles.

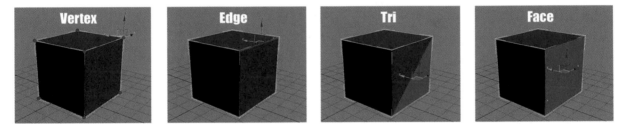

2.3 Components are the elements that make up polygonal geometry.

TRANSFORMATION TOOLS

Transformation is a generic term used to describe moving, rotating, or scaling an object or component. All of these functions are considered transforms. Almost everything you can select can be transformed using the same methods. Each software package is slightly different in its representation, but the idea is always the same. Not only will you be transforming objects as you model, but you'll also be transforming vertices, edges, faces, and even texture coordinates.

POLYGONS AND MEMORY

Polygons are a specific type of geometry. There are many ways to model, and several different types of geometry you can work with, including NURBS, subdivision surfaces, and patches. Polygons are the preferred type for games because polygons (also called tris) are made up entirely of triangles. Each face or polygon is made up of two triangles that share vertices. Most 3D software packages hide the edge that divides the face into triangles in order to keep things clean and easier to work with. Figure 2.4 presents a typical face that is divided into two triangles.

This information is simple and easy for a game engine to understand because for each triangle, all the engine needs to know is the x, y, and z values of its three points. NURBS geometry is more complex and is made up of mathematical curves. This is a great method for creating highly detailed objects and organic surfaces, and is what is typically used in film and broadcast-quality renders. However, the time it takes to render and calculate each curve is significant. A game engine can handle triangles much more efficiently than NURBS objects (at least for now!). Some game modelers like to create their geometry with NURBS or other methods and then convert to polygons. This method works, but typically takes extra time and may lead to a model that is less efficient and more difficult to work with. It contradicts our broad stroke principle!

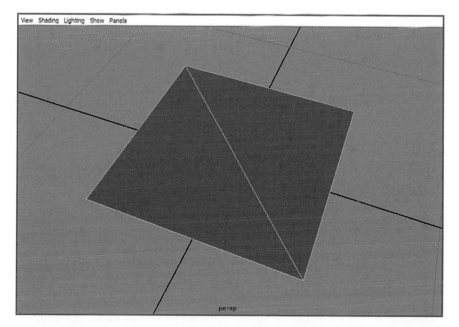

View Shading Lighting Show Panels

persp

2.4 A face composed of two triangles.

Box modeling, another term for polygonal modeling, is the most common and typically fastest way to produce game-ready geometry. Starting with a simple primitive, you transform components to extrude, cut, and sculpt it into your final product.

A game engine renders 3D geometry, textures, animation, and the like in essentially the same way a 3D software package does. But it is designed to do it very fast. To give you a point of comparison, when the movie *Toy Story* was released in late 1995, *each frame* of the movie took up to 15 hours to render. Each frame! A game engine typically renders between 30 and 60 frames *per second!* That means all geometry, textures, animation, sound, effects, and controller inputs are being processed and displayed in real-time, hence the term *real-time rendering.* Quite impressive. So, you can see the need to make your models and textures as efficient as possible in order to get as much detail on screen as possible. Of course, the faster computers get, the more information that can be processed per second, and the more detail a game can have. There seems to be a clear distinction in most people's minds between game art and traditional prerendered art, but as computing power increases exponentially, the line dividing the two is quickly disappearing.

With my experience working in both film and game environments, I have found that each has its own advantages and disadvantages. To me, the most appealing and exciting aspect of game art is the creative problem solving that needs to take place in order to create quality art. The challenge of overcoming limitations with your own creative mind is more rewarding to me than relying on the computer to do most of the work for you. Keep in mind, we are burdened with the stigma that games will never look as good as film. That idea is fading quickly, however.

Think about it this way. If you are rendering a specific shot for either a still image or a movie, you know exactly where the camera will be looking at all times. You don't have to worry about what is behind the tree or what the camera would see if it turned around 180 degrees. In games, you do. Your entire scene has to look great from any perspective. Knowing that the player has the ability to look everywhere at any time makes you approach your artwork in a very different way. No longer do you think about that one shot, but you think about the scene as a whole, solid piece of artwork. As of now, yes, game art can't quite hold itself up against a feature film. But, it won't be too long before a video game and a CG movie are virtually indistinguishable. Even some of the newest games on the market now are supporting an incredible amount of polygons as well as bump and specularity maps. Even real-time displacement maps! The next generation of hardware will make current polygon limits quite laughable.

As a game artist, another issue to take into consideration is that every time the power of real-time rendering increases, so does the amount of time it takes to make a game. To simplify the idea, imagine the time it takes to model and texture a car that is 500 polys versus a car that is 25,000 polys. Adding all that detail takes time. So the development of a game will inevitably take longer. On the other hand, game companies know that bigger doesn't always mean better. Consumers are currently comfortable with new games taking a year and a half to two years to develop before they hit the shelves. But five years ago, they were accustomed to a one-year turnaround at most. Companies are getting smarter about their development schedules and plans. They are starting projects with smaller, dedicated teams early enough to make something special that is released in accordance with consumer expectation. For example, *Metal Gear Solid 2: Sons of Liberty* took over three years to develop and is still one of the most complex and detailed games on the market.

It all comes down to memory, and making logical choices about how to spend it. We will be talking a lot about memory throughout the rest of this book, but I want you to start thinking about it now.

A good way to understand memory and how it affects the look of a game is to think about size. Let's compare two games, *Medal of Honor*™ and a fighting game like *Soul Caliber 2*. *Medal of Honor*™ has large-scale environments and sometimes up to 15 characters on screen at one time. A fighting game has one small environment that you never leave (the ring or arena) and two characters. Needless to say, the fighting game can look more detailed because you can use all your polygons and textures in one small place as opposed to spreading them out across a large world and dozens of characters. Both types of games will have the same memory limitations and amount of polygons on the screen, they just differ in how and where they use them.

POLYGON LIMITS

So how do you determine your limits? I think you can see how polygon limits are relative to the type of game or models you are creating. When a game is in preproduction, it's important to make estimates that are as realistic as possible. How many polygons should the character be? How many characters will there be? How large do the environments need to be? With these educated guesses in place, you begin to model and texture, pushing the limits until the game engine slows down. Then you go back for a poly reduction pass and clean everything up. Just remember, being smart about how you choose and use polys allows a great deal of apparent detail with a low number of actual polys. Figure 2.5 shows an example of a detailed-looking model that is built with a relatively small number of polygons.

You can see how much detail can be represented if you choose your polygons wisely.

2.5 A German E-boat from *Medal of Honor: Frontline* built with 1,300 polygons.

Medal of Honor Frontline™ IMAGES COURTESY OF ELECTRONIC ARTS INC. © 2002 ELECTRONIC ARTS INC. ALL RIGHTS RESERVED.

1300 Polygons

DISPLAYING POLYGON COUNT

While you are modeling, it's a good idea to keep your poly count information up and visible so you can monitor your progress. In Maya, go to Display>Heads Up Display>Poly Count. In 3ds max, go to the Utilities Menu. Click More, and select Polygon Counter. Figure 2.6 shows counts in both applications.

Keep in mind that the poly counts displayed here are for the same cube. 3ds max displays the number of triangles; in this case it is 432. In Maya, you will see the number of faces displayed, which is 216, exactly one half of 432. Why? You got it, because each face is two tris. So make sure that when your boss gives you a polygon limit, you verify whether you are both talking about the same thing!

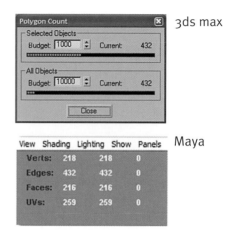

2.6 The Poly Count displays for 3ds max (top) and Maya (bottom).

NORMALS

There are two common types of normals in 3D geometry: face normals and vertex normals. (We'll discuss vertex normals more in Chapter 6, "Advanced Modeling.")

FACE NORMALS

Just as a vertex has its *xyz* coordinates in space, a face normal is another piece of information that is used to let the engine know what direction a face is facing so it can make an accurate decision on how to draw the face and how light and texture should be applied to it. Take a look at Figure 2.7, and you'll see the normals of a default cube. I've highlighted them in red for clarity.

Each normal points out of the face at a 90-degree angle from the face itself. This tells the engine how to draw the face. The reason that normals are so important to game art is that in most cases, you don't need a face to be double-sided. If the normal for a face is pointing away from the camera, the face will be invisible. As a matter of fact, most objects are by default one-sided. Let's look at it this way. One face is composed of two triangles and four vertices, right? When a face is double-sided, you suddenly have four triangles and eight vertices. As you can see, if your whole scene is double-sided, your polygon count is going to be rather large. The cube is a great example; we see the entire cube, but if we

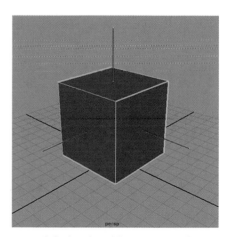

2.7 A default cube with its normals displayed. You can see how the faces with normals pointing toward the camera are displayed.

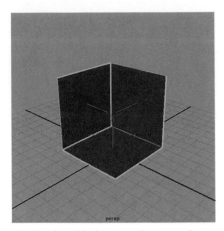

2.8 A cube with the normals reversed or flipped. Again, only the faces with normals facing the camera are shown.

were to get inside the cube and look out, you would see nothing. That's because each face has only one side, and they happen to be facing outward. Take a look at Figure 2.8. You can see the difference in a cube with the normals reversed.

Cases where you would choose to reverse normals might be if you are creating the interior of a room, or sometimes just to make working in 3D easier. As you begin to model and texture your scene in a game engine, you'll probably find some funky things happening to your geometry, like missing faces, black faces that should have a texture, and blinking faces. One of the first steps you should take in troubleshooting is to check your normals to make sure they are all facing the right direction.

To display normals in Maya, with the object selected, go to Display> Custom Polygon Display>Options, and check the Normals box (see Figure 2.9). You can also adjust the length of the normals that are displayed here. It helps to see them more clearly as you model.

In 3ds max, with the object selected, go into sub-object mode and choose Polygons. The option Show Normals will become available as a check box (see Figure 2.10).

2.9 Displaying normals in Maya.

Normals check box

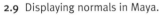

When working in a large scene and exporting to a game engine, you'll find that you have to flip normals quite often to get the result you are looking for. Even though we love to think of our 3D software as a stable and reliable environment to work in, it is still software, and there will always be bugs. When modeling, normals sometimes get flipped or reversed and you'll need to go back and correct the problem.

BACKFACE CULLING

Backface culling toggles the display of faces with normals that point away from the view. When on, you see through the wireframe to the backfaces. This applies only to wireframe viewports. Most software has backface culling on by default. Culling is a general term for "not drawing." Having backface culling off while modeling typically helps to keep your scene less cluttered and makes component selection easier. You can see the difference between a cube with backface culling on and off in Figure 2.11.

In Maya, with the object selected, go to Display>Custom Polygon Display>Options, and you will see a Backface Culling pulldown menu that lets you choose from a few options (see Figure 2.12).

In 3ds max, with the object selected, you can either right-click and choose Properties or go to Edit>Object Properties and check the Backface Cull check box (see Figure 2.13). You can also access this option in the Display menu in 3ds max.

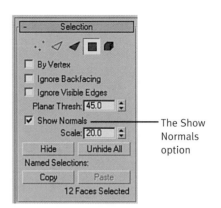

The Show Normals option

2.10 Displaying normals in 3ds max.

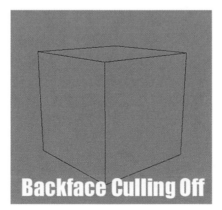

2.11 A cube with backface culling on and off.

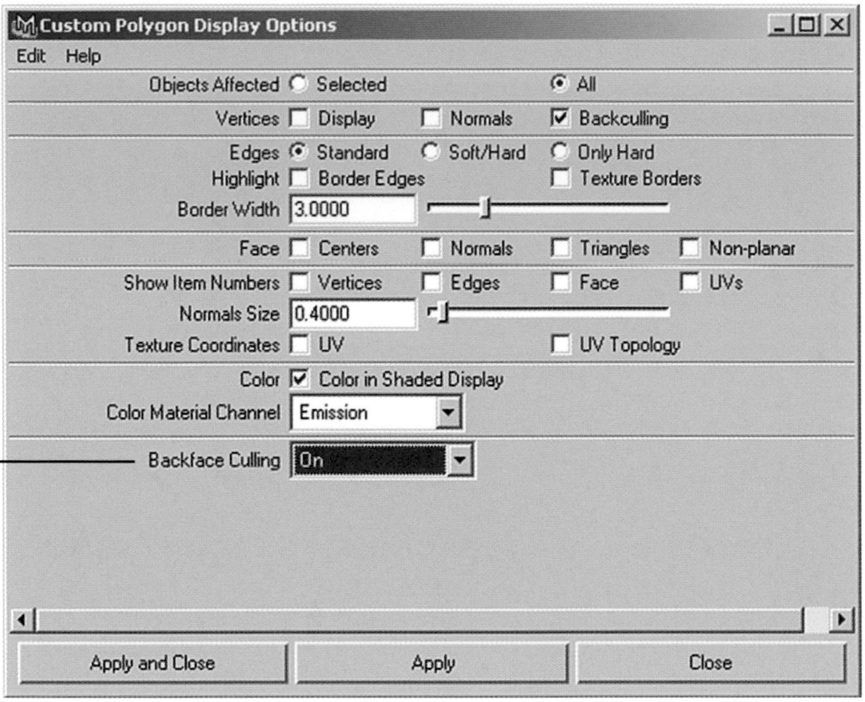

2.12 Backface culling in Maya.

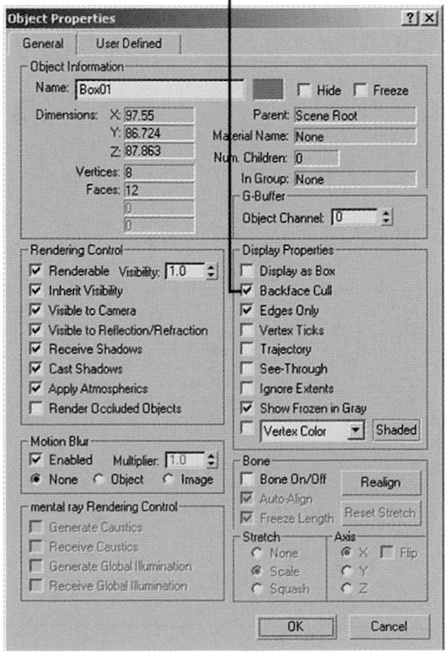

Backface Culling pulldown

Backface Cull option

2.13 Backface culling in 3ds max.

POLYGON REDUCTION

Being able to model efficiently without wasting polys takes some time and practice. The first step is to understand which polygons you need and which you don't. When modeling, ask yourself some of these questions:

- Will the player ever see this face? Imagine an oil barrel sitting on the ground; it's basically a cylinder. Can you see the face on the bottom of the barrel? Nope? Delete it.

- Are all these faces necessary? Your object might look great. Maybe there are some polys that you can see, but are they necessary to the model? Can you replace a 12-sided cylinder with an 8-sided one and have no visual impact? Yes? Do it.

- Is there tessellation that doesn't need to be there? Does the floor in a dark room have several subdivisions even though it's flat? Yes? Replace it with a simple two-poly plane.

Once you start to understand how and where to reduce, you will find yourself modeling much more efficiently. The process of low poly modeling usually involves a final pass on your models once everything is in place and final. Take a look at Figure 2.14. Look closely at the areas where the Mech has been reduced. Many pieces were replaced and compensated for with texture. The goal was to make the Mech look as good as possible without a ton of polys.

One of the best exercises you can do to get your head around poly reduction is to take a model and do everything you can to remove unnecessary faces and make it as efficient as possible.

Here is an exercise I give my students to learn the ropes of poly reduction. Understanding where polys can be removed helps in learning how to model efficiently in the first place.

Figure 2.15 contains a simple poly room with various props. It provides examples of situations you can expect to encounter when modeling and reducing geometry. The Maya file for this room is available on the web

76,000 polys

2000 polys

2.14 A comparison of a Mech before and after polygon reduction.

NOTE

You'll notice I reversed the faces of the room's shell so we can see inside.

site (http://www.peachpit.com/title/0753714096?redir=1) and is called Poly_room.mb. I suggest you download it and see how much you can reduce without sacrificing visual quality. The room is simple and already quite low poly, but there are many places where it can be reduced. The starting poly count is 722 faces. Before you read on, open the file and see what you can do to make it more efficient. The only geometry you cannot touch is the shell of the room (walls, floor, ceiling). The subdivisions that are there will need to stay for vertex lighting purposes.

With a little scrutiny, you can quickly see many areas of the room that can be reduced. I'll highlight a few of the key areas to point out common situations where faces can be removed. To demonstrate more clearly, I have used Maya's X-Ray mode (Shading>Shade Options> X-Ray).

Let's start with the tables. Each table still has faces at the end of each leg and under the table itself. None of these faces will ever be seen and should be deleted (see Figure 2.16).

In addition to that, because the table is in the corner and the player would only be able to see the table from one angle, we can remove faces from the backs and sides of the legs and table that will not be seen as

2.15 A simple polygon room.

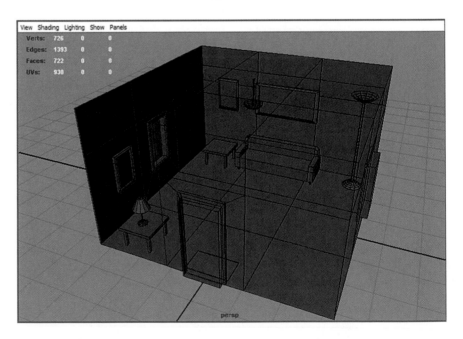

well (see Figure 2.17). You'll notice the couch, rug, and other table have the same types of faces that can be removed.

Now look at the windows and picture frames. One of the most obvious unnecessary faces in the one on the very top. Unless your character is 11 feet tall, it will never see the top of the window frame. Delete it!

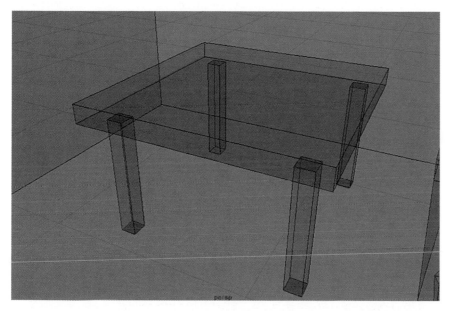

2.16 Faces on the ends of the table legs and under the tabletop itself can be removed.

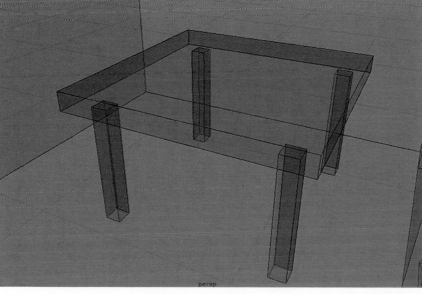

2.17 Think about the angle that the player will see the object from and remove faces accordingly.

If you look a little closer, you'll find some faces in the frame that might have escaped your first glance. These types of faces can be created unintentionally in the modeling process, so it's a good idea to keep an eye out for them as you work (see Figure 2.18).

And now for the lamp. The lamp can be reduced in several ways. First things first, there are extra faces on both ends of the central cylinder (see Figure 2.19). Bye-bye.

2.18 Remove the top edge and the extra faces that were created during the modeling process.

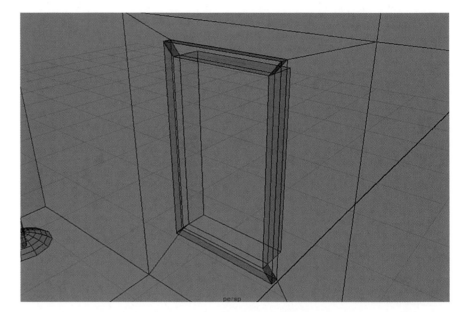

2.19 Remove the end caps of the central cylinder.

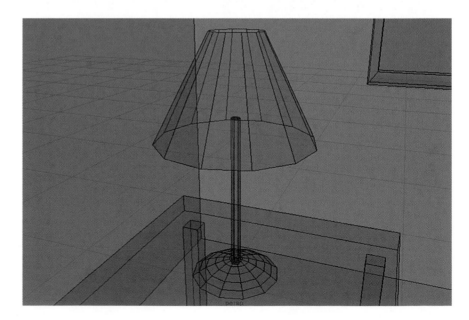

Next, we need to look at the lamp and realize that overall there is more detail in the lamp than there needs to be. This is a situation in which we might want to replace certain elements with more simple geometry. The central cylinder has six sides. Considering the actual size of the lamp, this cylinder could easily be three sides and still look the same. The base of the lamp is also more complex than it really needs to be. Although the number of sides looks right, the number of horizontal divisions can be reduced to save polys. Faces can also be deleted where the base meets the central cylinder. The final product can be seen in Figure 2.20. You can do the same with the lamp that is hanging from the ceiling.

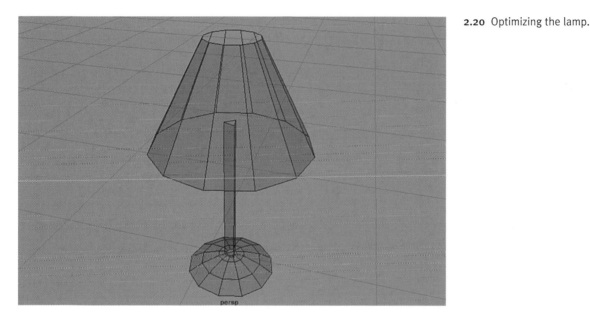

2.20 Optimizing the lamp.

There are plenty of places where the room can be reduced. See if you can get it down below 400 faces without affecting the visual integrity.

MODELING TECHNIQUES

All right, now that you have an understanding of what makes for an efficient model, let's talk about how to build objects correctly from scratch. As I mentioned before, there are endless ways to reach your final goal. In this section I'm going to point out a few methods I have found that can help you get off on the right foot.

To be perfectly honest, I really think the term *low-poly modeling* is inaccurate; *creative modeling* is a much more precise term. Sure, low-poly modeling was appropriate several years ago, when a character could not be more than 500 polys. But now, it's all about modeling with polygons in an efficient and productive way. And I can't tell you how much joy comes with producing a solid and reliable model or scene that looks great and holds up within the limitations of a real-time environment. For those of you who have been modeling with NURBS or other methods, you'll find that polygon modeling can be more intuitive and engaging than taking all the shortcuts and hacks necessary to produce one shot in a film. Many artists are migrating toward games not only because of the obvious opportunities in the gaming industry, but also because of the satisfaction of having more creative control over their individual artwork. Even film production has been gradually moving toward this philosophy in recent years.

Game modeling often involves a lot of extruding, subdividing and cutting faces, and what I like to call vertex surgery. Vertex surgery is the careful crafting of your vertices until you get the desired result. Although it may sound tedious, you'll be surprised at how quick and simple polygonal modeling can be.

No matter the software, you can count on certain tools and techniques that you will find you are using 80–90% of the time. Learn these tools and you'll have everything you need to model virtually anything you can imagine.

EXTRUDE

Extrusion is probably the most common tool you can expect to use when modeling with polygons. Extruding basically means taking a component (more often than not, a face) and duplicating it, pulling, pushing, or scaling it to extend or refine the model. To give the simplest example, Figure 2.21 presents a cube that has had one of its faces extruded outward and scaled down.

Extruding has hundreds of uses. It can be used to extend or expand your model, create appendages, or even define areas like windows and doors. Here is a quick demonstration on using extrude to make a window on a building.

> **NOTE**
>
> In Maya you can find Extrude in the Edit Geometry box under the Modify panel. In 3ds max you'll find Extrude under the Modify tab when you have a face selected.

1. Select a face.

   Extrude and scale to the size of the window you want, keeping it flush with the rest of the wall (see Figure 2.22).

2. Extrude again, and this time push the face back into the wall (see Figure 2.23).

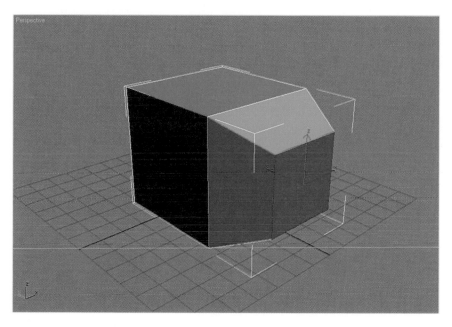

2.21 The face of a cube extruded outward and scaled down.

2.22 Extruding and scaling a face to create the window size.

3. Now if you want a frame on the window, select the newly created faces around the border and extrude them outward (see Figure 2.24).

This technique works great for doors, alcoves, and other features of buildings.

2.23 Extruding again recesses the face back into the wall.

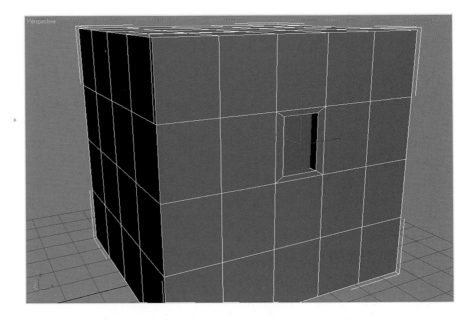

2.24 Adding a window frame is as easy as extruding the newly created faces outward.

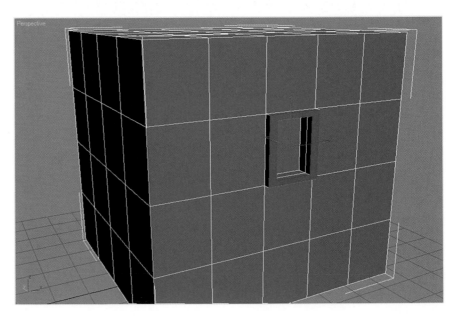

THE LINE TOOL

The line tool is extremely useful and artist friendly because it allows you to draw the outline of an object or character and then extrude that outline into a three-dimensional shape. The line tool is most useful in situations where you need an exact representation of the object you are modeling. There is some risk involved with starting your model this way in that you can easily create vertices and faces that are not necessary. It's easy to get carried away and click in a bunch of verts that might not be necessary. But, if you take your time to think about how it will all come together, you'll find this method very easy and productive. One good example of where the line tool becomes valuable is when you need to define a contour with precision. Let's say you are modeling a certain type of car. You do your research and collect references that give you a side view of the vehicle. Import that image into a side viewport using the methods described in Chapter 1, and using the line tool, you can plot out the vertices and extrude the general shape of the car (see Figure 2.25).

Another option for modeling a vehicle like this would be to use the box modeling technique. I prefer this method because of the broad stroke theory that I'm sure you are tired of hearing about by now! But by starting with a solid and reliable primitive, the integrity of your model is more insured and understandable.

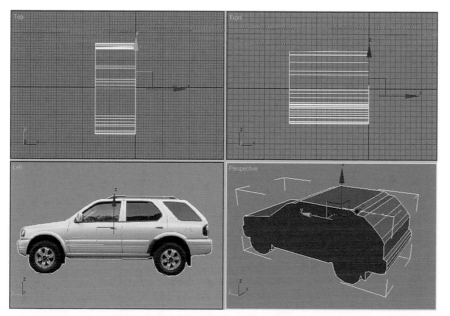

2.25 Using the line tool to define the general shape of the car.

1. Start by creating a simple primitive box (see Figure 2.26).

2. Next, extrude outward to fit the general size of the vehicle. Create enough subdivisions to block out the major angles and contours (see Figure 2.27).

3. Finally, move your verts and tweak until you get the general shape (see Figure 2.28).

2.26 A simple primitive box.

2.27 Extrude outward to create enough subdivisions.

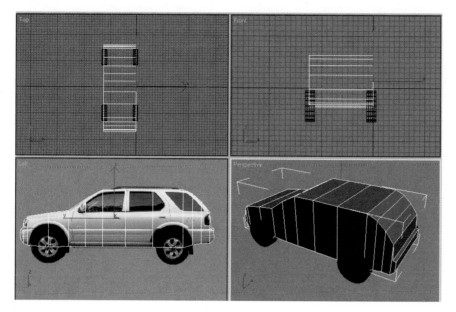

Now you've got a solid piece of geometry to work with!

COMMON MISTAKES

There are a few no-nos when modeling for export to a game engine. Keep in mind that what you see in your 3D software will be quite different from what you see when you export to a game engine. What you see is what you get is typically not the norm when working in games. It's not necessarily a bad thing. Once you learn and can predict the result of an engine's rendering, you'll quickly adapt to the requirements and specifics of that game engine. Regarding all the following modeling issues, a good practice is to model with your triangle edges visible. It will help you identify problems and see mistakes you may not catch when they are hidden.

OVERLAPPING FACES

Overlapping faces are a common problem in polygonal modeling. They typically occur when you are duplicating or combining geometry. An overlapping face is a face that is sitting on top of another. Not only is it a waste of verts, but it also can cause visual problems like z-fighting and lighting issues. You can usually see overlapping faces as a flashing or flickering when you move around the geometry. Welding or merging vertices on your model is the best solution. But keep an eye out for faces that look like those in Figure 2.29.

2.29 Overlapping faces look inconsistent and will flicker when you move the camera around them.

T-Junctions

As game engines become more advanced, T-junctions are becoming less of an issue. But they can easily cause a lot of strange seams and holes when you export, even though they may look fine in the 3D viewport. A T-junction occurs when an edge does not share a vertex with another edge. It causes subtle and almost unnoticeable slivers in geometry that can cause not only visual problems, but also issues with collision and surface detection. T-junctions should be avoided at all cost, especially if the cost is the addition of even a single vertex. Figure 2.30 shows an example of T-junctions.

Stray Vertices

Closely tied to T-junctions are stray vertices. When you create a T-junction, it will often create a stray vert that is floating in space. This is wasteful and can cause similar visual issues to T-junctions: sliced geometry, collision problems, and other unpredictable effects. The best way to avoid stray verts and T-junctions is, of course, careful modeling. But you should always be using your software's tools to weld or merge vertices to be sure the model is as solid as possible.

If you have to use these additional edges, it would be more acceptable to have something like what is shown in Figure 2.31, where every edge shares a vertex and nothing is floating out on its own.

This leads us to our next no-no that can create unintentional extra faces, edges, and vertices.

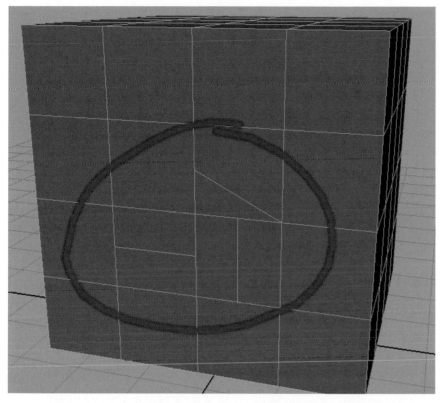

2.30 T-junctions can cause multiple problems. Avoid them!

2.31 When every edge shares a vertex, you'll have a much more stable model.

STAR-LIKE FACES

Star-like faces or "fans" can cause a lot of problems, ranging from messed up normal smoothing to normals that are inconsistent. Other typical side effects are texturing problems, streaky and inconsistent lighting, and flipped or missing faces. This goes back to the need to keep your models as clean and grid-like as possible. Trust me, at first it's easier to create fast and sloppy models than to take the time necessary to think ahead and do it right. But that's what makes the difference between a successful and a mediocre game artist. Figure 2.32 shows star-like faces and the thin triangles they create.

Again, modeling with your triangle edges visible will help you avoid these situations as you work. Starting with simple primitives and continually merging vertices will also assist in keeping your model clean.

2.32 Star-like faces or "fans" can cause thin and problematic triangles.

CONCLUSION

Now that you understand the limitations and logic behind polygonal modeling for games, we can move on to the *really* good stuff! Even though the chapters in this book are clearly separated into specific focuses, I want you to be thinking about modeling, texturing, and lighting as parts of the whole. As you move through this book, I hope that you will start to realize how all these pieces have to work together. As you model, you need to be thinking down the line as to how you plan to texture and light the objects you are creating. Why add a detail with geometry if it can be represented better and more cheaply with a texture? Whether you will be doing all the work yourself or handing the model off to a texture or lighting artist, it's beneficial to think about the entire package and work with the final product in mind. It will save you and everyone involved a lot of time and make the entire process enjoyable and productive. So, let's move on next to talk about texturing!

INTRODUCTION TO TEXTURING

CREATING TEXTURES FOR GAMES is one of the most challenging, yet rewarding, aspects of game art. As a texture artist, you are responsible for defining the surface characteristics and detail of all the objects in your scene. When compared with texturing for high-resolution renders, game textures require a bit more attention and thought to achieve the desired result. You typically have specific limitations in a game environment, so you have to take the extra time to be sure you are texturing as efficiently and effectively as possible. You may be asked to create composite textures that are essentially several textures condensed together into one image that is then applied to the entire model—a process you would not need to do when texturing for a high-res render. You'll also find that you need to paint details into your textures to compensate for lower polygon geometry. For these reasons, texturing for games takes a bit of extra thought and creativity.

In order to better understand the process of texturing, it's important to make a clear distinction between a texture and a shader. Shaders

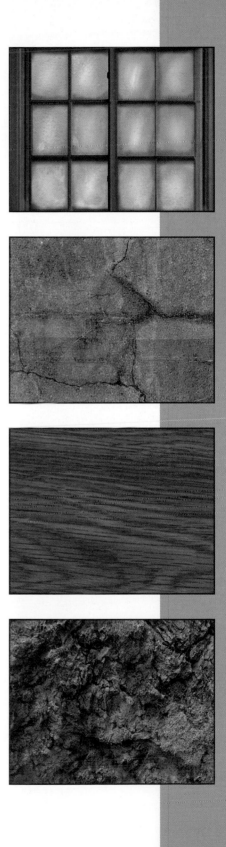

(also called materials) define the surface properties of an object—how shiny it is, how bumpy it might be, how lights affect the object, and so on. A texture is simply the bitmap that is plugged into the shader that defines the image we want to appear on the object. For a long time, using shaders or materials in a game was unheard of. Objects were given a simple texture that was then mapped onto the geometry with no shading network or surface properties associated with it. Now the opportunity to use complex materials and truly define the surface of your objects is becoming much more commonplace. Even though many games are already using bump, specularity, displacement, and the like, their use is still somewhat limited in a real-time environment. We'll discuss shaders and other types of maps in detail in the next chapter. The important thing to keep in mind when texturing for games is that with the obvious restrictions of a real-time environment, we rely heavily on texture to sell our scene. Having these limitations simply means that the artist has to find creative solutions to compensate for the restrictions.

Games rely heavily on texture to establish the detail and realism of a scene. The challenge of working with lower resolution, reuse, and tiling may seem intimidating at first, but I think you'll find the opportunity for creative problem solving is what makes texturing such an enjoyable and rewarding process.

This chapter will focus on the theory and process of creating effective and beautiful textures for games. Technical limitations aside, choosing the right texture will make the difference between an average and an exceptional scene.

GAME TEXTURING THEORY

The secret to creating great textures is taking the time to think about the *story behind the object*. It's not just about learning which filters to use in Photoshop or how to take the best digital photo. Producing engaging textures takes thought. You need to consider the object's purpose, its environment, and what elements affect it. Taking that extra bit of time to truly think about what you can do to accentuate the texture will take your scene to the next level.

Assuming that your team has gone through the process of collecting references, creating concept art, and defining the art direction of the game, you should have the information you need to start collecting and painting textures.

Let's discuss an example. Let's say that we are modeling and texturing a door for a building. Now, some people might just take a picture of a door, or find one on the Internet that looks cool, and slap it on their model. Not us. For an actor or a writer, the more that is known about a character's past, personality, experiences, likes and dislikes, and so on, the more believable the character will be. The same is true with 3D art. We need to know as much as possible about this door before we begin. So we ask ourselves some questions.

- What material is it? Wood? If so, what type?
- How old is the door?
- Who uses it?
- Which way does it swing open?
- Has it been repainted? If so, what colors? How long ago?
- What else can we add or exaggerate in order to make it more interesting?

I think you get the idea. Look at the two textures shown in Figures 3.1 and 3.2.

Grunge has been added in areas where the door is most used. For example, the areas around the doorknob and in the region where someone might knock show signs of heavy use. Scarring has been added toward the bottom where shoes or other objects are likely to bump into the door, leaving marks and scratches of various colors. I've also accentuated shadow around the edges and top to give it more depth.

Looking at the before and after of the door, which is more interesting to look at? Which will be more intriguing to players in a game environment?

It's a way of thinking that gives you the information you need as an artist to make something interesting and realistic.

DETAIL IN TEXTURE

Because real-time rendering requires a limited amount of geometry, texture is used to compensate for the details that cannot be represented with polygons. It becomes the responsibility of the texture artist to define the details of the scene.

Figure 3.3 presents an example of how texture can add depth to plain geometry.

3.1 A simple white door, in good condition.

3.2 The same door with some thought put into it.

3.3 A simple box with a texture that adds detail.

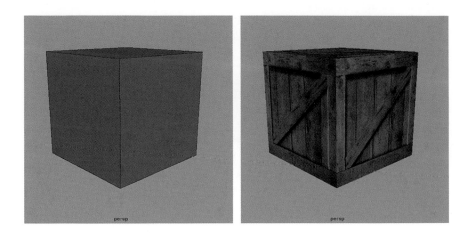

Even though the box itself is only 12 polygons and flat on the sides, you can create the illusion that there is more complexity to the object just by choosing an appropriate texture.

How to Choose and Create Textures

A texture is rarely ready to go right out of the box. It's tempting to grab an image online or scan one from a book and assign it to your model. Whenever I begin texturing an object, no matter the situation, my textures always spend some time in Photoshop for a little pampering and customization before they are applied to the model. Maybe it's as simple as adjusting the brightness and contrast, or as in depth as adding and painting 20 new layers. As long as we know we are going to spend some quality time with the texture, we need to think about what we can do to make it more interesting to look at.

If you start to think about each texture, whether it's a coffee mug or a building façade, as an individual piece of artwork, you will end up with the most realistic and professional-looking scene. All the objects in your environment have to feel as if they belong there. All too often, things are thrown together without going through this simple thought process, and the result is a haphazard, disjointed environment. Again, you'll make drastically different decisions about what this texture looks like if you think of each texture as an individual piece of artwork in addition to it being a part of the harmonious whole. Figures 3.4 through 3.6 illustrate a few before and afters.

You can see that giving the texture a little more attention to detail makes it all the more appealing. It's important to remember, however, that if you know that a specific texture is going to be tiled or reused, it's

3.4 The wood on the right is less saturated and has interesting markings like scratches, nicks, and a coffee mug stain.

3.5 The window on the right has more depth and keeps your attention longer because of the added detail.

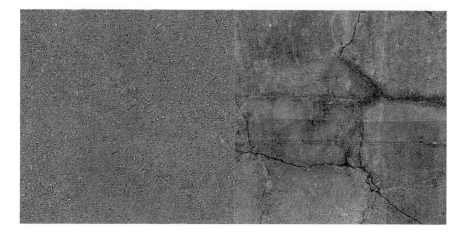

3.6 If you are going to make concrete, make it interesting!

best to avoid painting in obvious details because they will be very apparent when you tile. Repeating textures need to be a bit more uncharacteristic for that reason.

FILE FORMATS

There are dozens of different file formats, each one designed for specific reasons with its own advantages and disadvantages. Before we talk about game-specific formats, let's talk about what a bitmap really is. To start, there are two types of images: bitmap and vector. Bitmap images are made up of pixels—small dots of color that make up the whole image. A bitmap is the typical format for use in programs like Photoshop and Painter. A bitmap image, which is resolution dependent, causes the image to degrade the more you zoom in, but can accurately represent any type of image including digital photographs. Formats that you are probably most familiar with are bitmap formats such as JPEG, GIF, Targa, and BMP.

A vector image is a series of shapes and colors generated mathematically. The result is a very clean and geometric image. The biggest advantage of a vector image is that it is resolution independent. You can draw a circle and zoom in on it 100 times, and the image will never degrade. Vector images also tend to produce smaller file sizes. Common vector-based software packages include Adobe Illustrator and Macromedia Flash. The downside to vector images is that they are composed of mathematically generated shapes and colors, so it is difficult to represent a realistic photograph in that format. Common Vector formats are AI (Adobe Illustrator files) and SWF (Shockwave Files). Vector images can be imported into most 3D programs and can actually be used as curves with which to model. For example, you can import vector text and extrude it into 3D geometry.

Some file formats most commonly used for games are:

- TGA (Targa) 32 bit
- TIFF (Tagged Image File Format) 32 bit
- PNG (Portable Network Graphics)
- BMP (Windows bitmap)

Each game engine typically has its own file format that it understands best. Many have compression. But for the most part, as a game artist, the conversion to that engine's format will happen behind the scenes, and the files you produce will most likely be TGAs.

COLOR DEPTH

The following is a list of color depths (sometimes called color resolution or bit depth). High-resolution and high-color-depth textures look the best, but slow game performance. It's important to choose a size and color depth that offer the best possible quality with acceptable performance.

The depths listed in **bold** are the most commonly used. Color depths like 3, 5, 6, and 7 are byte alignment unfriendly, which simply means that they do not work well in memory.

1 bit = 2 colors

2 bit = 4 colors

3 bit = 8 colors

4 bit = 16 colors

5 bit = 32 colors

6 bit = 64 colors

7 bit = 128 colors

8 bit = 256 colors

16 bit = 65,536 colors

24 bit = 16,777,215 colors

32 bit = 16,777,215 colors + an 8-bit alpha channel

RESOLUTION (TEXTURE SIZE)

When creating art for games, get used to working in multiples of 2. We discussed in the previous section that odd color depths don't work well in memory. Well, the same is true for texture sizes that don't fall into the following specifications. Here are the common texture resolutions:

32×32

64×32

64×64

128×64

128×128

256×128

256×256

512×256

512×512

1024×1024

3.7 15 rocks.

3.8 30 rocks.

3.9 Sand.

Even though these texture sizes have perfectly square or rectangular aspect ratios, more recent console and PC hardware support different sizes and dimensions. Textures that are powers of two are also increasingly accepted and supported. However, they are generally slower to render and should be avoided.

WHAT IS RESOLUTION?

Imagine someone handed you 15 rocks, each the size of your fist, and asked you to arrange them on the ground to make a smiley face. You might get something like what is shown in Figure 3.7.

It looks a little like a smiley face, but it is a bit hard to make out.

Now imagine you were given 30 slightly smaller rocks and asked to do the same thing (see Figure 3.8).

Much better, but still not as clear as we would like.

Now, imagine you have a large bag of fine, granulated sand with which to accomplish the same task (see Figure 3.9).

The smiley face is now clear and detailed.

The idea of resolution is very similar. The more rocks (pixels) you have to work with, the more detailed and accurate your image will be.

Another way to think about resolution would be to compare it to a traditional painting. Imagine you are painting on a canvas that is 18"×24". Now picture a canvas the size of an entire wall! The amount of detail you can put into the painting is increased dramatically.

PHOTOSHOP

In my opinion, Adobe Photoshop is the most robust and refined digital imaging program available. The majority of the computer graphics software on the market today is based in some way on the ideas that were first established in Photoshop. Photoshop is still one of the most powerful, stable, and productive software packages in the industry.

For the purposes of this book, I will assume you have had some experience using Photoshop, but I still want to go over a few common procedures.

IMAGE RESIZING

Resizing an image is a fairly simple procedure. Let's walk through the process using an example.

1. Open Grass.tga from the files you downloaded from the book's page on the New Riders web site (see Figure 3.10).

2. The figure's resolution is 512×512. We can verify and change that number by using the Image Size command. You can access this command either from the Image menu or by right-clicking on the top bar of the image. In the dialog box that appears, you can see the size and resolution information for this particular image. To change the size, type "256" into the top window. If you know that you want to keep the image the same proportion, check the Constrain Proportions box (see Figure 3.11).

3. Now click OK, and the image will be resized.

3.10 A simple grass texture.

3.11 The Image Size window.

NOTE

When you shrink an image, you often lose some quality and will sometimes get a slightly blurred image. Use the Unsharp Mask Filter in Photoshop to compensate for this.

When gathering and creating textures, it's always a good idea to save your images at as large a resolution as possible. You only want to shrink them when it's time to actually put them into the game engine. Another good reason for keeping your images at a high resolution is that as you start to develop a texture library of your own (sometimes called a morgue); you never know when you might want to reuse a texture down the road. And who knows how high of a resolution you'll be able to use on the PlayStation 5!

WHERE DO I USE MY PIXELS?

One of the challenges in texturing for video games is that you need to create textures that end up being relatively low resolution (larger and fewer rocks to work with) while trying to make the scene look as detailed as possible. The bottom line is, with the memory limitations of real-time rendering, you have a set number of pixels with which to make your game. The trick is to make intelligent decisions about where to use those pixels.

Two important aspects to think about when choosing the resolution of a texture are:

■ Physical size—The actual size of the object in relation to a character.

■ Distance—How far away is the object and how close can the player get to it?

Here is another example: Let's say we are texturing a small room with a cardboard box on the floor, a clock on the wall, and a window that shows a lighthouse in the distance (see Figure 3.12).

How big should the textures be for each of the elements in the scene? Let's break it down.

What is the largest element in the scene that the player could get close to? The wall is an element, and the player could walk directly up to it. In this case, a 512×512 texture should do the trick (see Figure 3.13).

Now, let's look at the clock. It's a relatively small object and is quite high up on the wall. We can definitely use a smaller texture, keeping in mind that textures that have text (and/or photos) typically need to be a slightly higher resolution so we can read and understand them. In this case, a 64×64 texture should work well (see Figure 3.14).

The cardboard box is sitting on the floor and is only about two-feet square. Now, unless the player were to duck down and crawl right up to it (for the purposes of this exercise, let's say the player can only walk

3.12 Our example room.

upright), you don't get very close to it, and its physical size is not big enough to justify a large texture. A 128×128 texture will be perfect (see Figure 3.15).

The floor can actually be a small texture that is tiled several times. (We'll discuss tiling more as we move through the book.) We'll use a 128×128 texture and tile it three times in each direction (see Figure 3.16).

Even though a lighthouse is typically quite a large object, in this scene, it is far in the distance. From the player's point of view, it's a relatively small object in the scene. We can get away with a 32×64 texture and still get a good-looking lighthouse (see Figure 3.17).

As you can see, there is no exact science to choosing what resolution to use in each case. One way to ensure that you are making good choices is to make sure that all the objects in your scene maintain a consistent overall pixel resolution in the environment. Imagine you have two textures that are right next to one another. It's important to make sure that both textures have about the same pixel resolution. Look at Figure 3.18. You can see that the texture on the right looks stretched and blurry in comparison because it does not contain as many pixels as the one on the left. In Figure 3.19 you see a more-balanced pixel resolution. Looking at your scene from this point of view will help you make better choices regarding which resolution to choose.

3.13 The wall is an important element in the scene. We'll use a 512×512 texture.

3.14 Textures that have text need to be a bit larger to keep them legible.

3.15 The cardboard box works well at 128×128.

3.16 A tilable floor texture.

3.17 Because the lighthouse is so far in the distance, we can get away with a smaller texture. In this case, 32×64 is perfect.

3.18 Two textures with drastically different pixel resolutions.

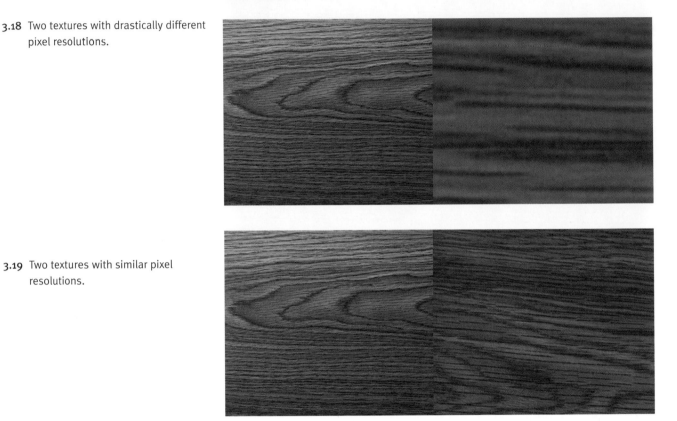

3.19 Two textures with similar pixel resolutions.

You can now start to see that choosing the right resolution for a texture is just like deciding how many polys to use when modeling an object. Once you start to keep these guidelines in mind, your work will become more efficient and easy to work with. Video games aside, even for prerendered work, the idea of managing your texture resolutions is the same. You'll have faster renders and a much more efficient and easy to navigate scene if you manage your texture resolutions in this way.

CHANGING COLOR DEPTH

Changing color depth is also an important factor in optimizing your textures. A bitmap with 16 colors takes up a lot less memory than a bitmap with 65,536 colors. I always test a texture at a lower color depth to see if it holds up well enough. You'd be surprised at how much you can save by reducing the amount of color in an image. In certain cases, having less color is advantageous from a visual standpoint as well.

For example, in *Medal of Honor*™, we were going for a very desaturated, washed-out look (see Figure 3.20). The idea behind this was that people tend to associate World War II with black and white or low quality color footage. If you watch *Saving Private Ryan*, you'll notice that there is not much color in the movie. Because we knew that we were not going to have tons of vibrant colors in the game, we made the majority of our textures 4 bit (16 colors). This actually helped give the game its unique look, and at the same time, nearly tripled the amount of textures we could have in the game due to the memory we saved.

There are several ways to change color depth in Photoshop. When you save an image in a specific format like TGA or TIFF, you'll be prompted to choose a color depth of 16, 24, or 32 bits per pixel. But what if you want to save as 4 bit (16 color)?

Let's change the color depth of the image grass.tga from 24 bit to 4 bit:

1. Open the bitmap in Photoshop. Go to the Image menu, select Mode, and then choose Indexed Color.

2. You'll be prompted to choose from several options. I always use Local (Perceptual). This option chooses colors based on how they appear on screen and will give you the most accurate representation of your original colors. In the color field, type 16. Keep the Forced option set to None. Forcing colors adds colors to your palette that may not be necessary. Also be sure that Transparency is not checked. It will also add unnecessary information to your image (see Figure 3.21).

3.20 A screenshot from *Medal of Honor Frontline*™.

3.21 Changing color depth.

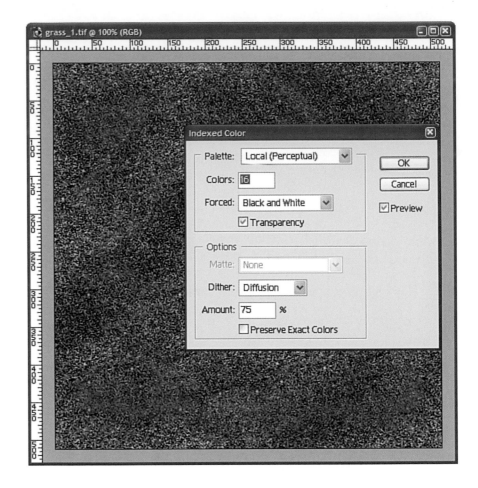

MORE ABOUT COLOR

A common mistake in computer graphics (CG) when trying to render realistically is too much saturation. The key to creating believable CG is to hide the fact that the images you are seeing were generated by a computer. This is more difficult than it seems. Color plays a big part in this deception. If you can, turn on your TV for a moment. Flip through the channels looking at nothing but the overall colors on each channel. Now look at your computer's desktop, and compare the two. You'll notice that the colors on the TV are very muted and desaturated in comparison to the computer. Even the colors you see walking around outside or in your house are muted in comparison. There is a tendency to take colors to their max when working on the computer. In fact, you'll almost never see a true 255,0,0 (pure RGB red) in the real world.

Not to mention the fact that a TV screen has a much lower resolution than a computer monitor and cannot display nearly as many colors.

A TV's resolution is 720×486. Most computers are 1024×768 or higher, and are capable of producing literally millions of colors. Toning down the colors in your scene will usually give you a much more realistic and believable look. If you are developing a game for a console that will be displayed on a TV, you have to make some adjustments to take this into account. For those of you who have created 3D work and dropped it onto a videotape to watch on a TV, you'll know why we joke that NTSC stands for "never the same color."

Colors that are vibrant and saturated on your computer monitor explode when they get on TV—even more so on VHS. Reds bleed and blur, and whites blow out (and can even cause sound distortion!). When games are developed for multiple platforms or ported from a PC to a PS2, Gamecube, or Xbox, the saturation of the textures has to be reduced, sometimes up to 50% of what they were on the PC, in order to look right on TV. Although a TV typically doesn't yield as crisp an image as a computer monitor, using connections like component or S-video significantly increase the quality of the image. But when making console games, it's important to remember that not everyone has a perfectly new TV and the proper connections. It's your responsibility as an artist to be sure the game looks as good as it can in any situation.

Digital Photography

A digital camera is, without question, one of the best investments a digital artist can make. Work purposes aside, having a camera that has essentially unlimited film and doesn't cost anything to develop is a great thing. But for the purposes of taking photos for reference or textures, it is an extremely valuable tool. We've broken this topic down into two sections: digital photos for reference and digital photos for textures.

Digital Photos for Reference

If you plan to go on a photo shoot to take broad pictures for use as reference, try to go into the adventure with some prior knowledge. Let's say you are building a redwood forest and need some reference. So you do your research and find out where to go, and get your camera ready. Remember to bring these things:

- A tripod—The best way to take a clear digital photograph is to have the camera mounted on a tripod and use the self-timer option so you can be sure there will be no movement to blur the image. This is especially important when taking photos for textures.

- Memory and batteries—Bring more memory and batteries than you think you need. Every time I've been on a photo shoot, I've always wished I had more to work with. I know they are both expensive, but see if your friends may be willing to loan you what you need for the day.

- Video camera—It's great to capture the essence of the environment: sounds, movement, atmosphere. Not to mention the fact that you can take any frame from the video and maybe catch the image that eluded you.

- Lens cloth—You'll be very angry if you take a ton of great shots and discover later that the lens was dirty.

- A disposable or other film camera—A good backup, and at times, the only way to capture a certain image. Even though digital cameras are capable of taking high-resolution images, it's important to remember that it is a different format than film. Film cameras can often capture subtleties and lighting that digital cannot.

Digital Photos for Textures

The most important point to remember when taking digital pictures for textures is lighting. The best time to take texture pictures is when it's overcast because you have light, but no direct light source. Imagine you take a beautiful picture of a tree on a sunny day at 5 p.m. The lighting may be dramatic and beautiful, but let's say you get back to work the next day and realize that your scene doesn't have any direct sun, or is at night. Maybe the sun is out but the time in your scene is 12:00 noon, and the sun is directly above you. Without a lot of extra work in Photoshop, which will surely degrade your image, you have an unusable texture. So it is very important to know your scene's information before you go on a shoot, and it's always the best choice to take photos that are neutral in light source and are practical for multiple uses in the future. As I mentioned earlier, using a tripod and self-timer are ideal. I find that in cases where I don't have my tripod with me, I try to set the camera down on a stable surface and use the self-timer, as opposed to pressing the shutter myself, to minimize any blurring. I also take the photo at the highest resolution, knowing that I can always crop if I need to.

MAKING A TEXTURE TILABLE

There are many ways to make a texture repeat (tile), sometimes called a seamless texture. The advantage to tiling is that you can use one texture that repeats to cover a large area while keeping resolution. Taking advantage of any opportunity to reuse textures is a good idea. The types of textures that are commonly tiled or repeated are for large areas of the same type, such as grass, concrete, walls, streets, and dirt. The risk is that you will see the repeating pattern across your geometry. Repetition is one of my pet peeves. I can't stand to see repetition in games, whether it be in a texture or seeing the same building over and over again on the same street. That doesn't mean it can't be there, you just have to find ways to hide it. We'll get into that more in Chapter 4, "Advanced Texturing." Let's start by talking about how you can make a tilable texture.

The most commonly used tool for tiling is a filter in Photoshop called Offset (Filter>Other>Offset). You can make an image seamless by wrapping the image. For example, let's say you have a 512×512 image. Choose the Offset Filter and enter 256 for both the horizontal and vertical fields. Make sure that the Wrap Around option is selected. This will turn your image inside out in order to make the edges match up. You'll be left with seams in the center of the image. Using the Clone Brush, paint over the seams until the image looks solid. This method works well for many images, but here is a trick to creating seamless textures that gives the artist a bit more control. It's actually very simple and lets you make the choices.

1. Open the image Rock_mossy.tga in Photoshop (see Figure 3.22).

   Figure 3.23 shows the texture tiled twice. You can clearly see the seams where the texture repeats. The trick is to remove the seams without taking away the characteristics of the image.

2. Using the selection marquee, copy and paste about a 75-pixel selection from the left-hand side of the image (see Figure 3.24).

3. Now, with this part on its own layer, use free transform (Ctrl+T) and mirror the layer (see Figure 3.25).

   To accurately move it over to the other side of the figure, make sure you have either Snap to Document Bounds checked (View>Snap To>Document Bounds) or guides in place to ensure you have proper alignment. Move the piece over to the other side until it snaps into place. Now we know that the two sides will match perfectly when their edges meet in a tile (see Figure 3.26).

3.22 Rock_mossy.tga.

3.23 A nontiling texture.

3.24 Copy and paste a selection from one side of the image.

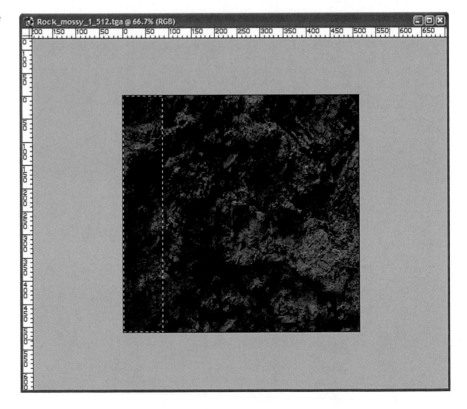

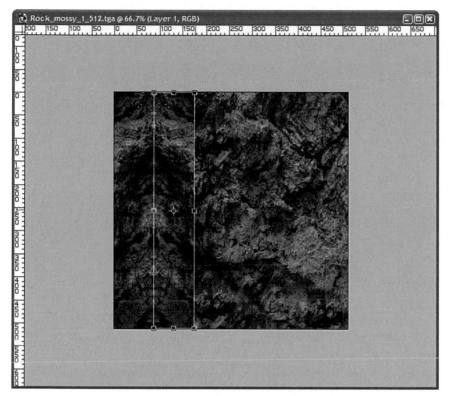

3.25 Free transform.

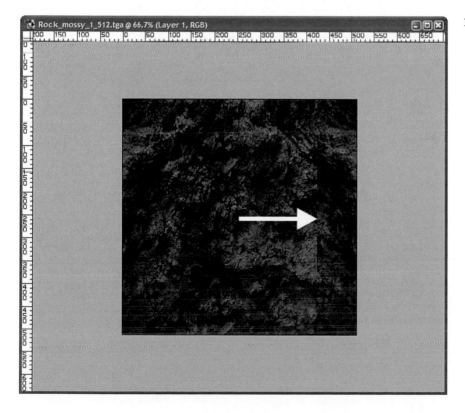

3.26 Now the left and right edges are the same.

> **TIP**
>
> A great keyboard shortcut for this is to use the number keys; for example, if you want 50% opacity, you can just tap the 5 key. If you need a specific number like 53, just type 53 quickly.

> **TIP**
>
> To control the brush size, hit the bracket keys ([]) to increase or decrease size. Use the Shift key with the bracket keys to control the hardness or softness of the brush.

4. The next step is to blend the piece with the rest of the image. Select the Eraser tool (or a layer mask), and choose a brush that has a soft edge. Reduce the opacity of that brush to about 50%.

5. Now you can erase the majority of the top layer, keeping only the areas towards the edge (which we know lines up perfectly) and blending the two layers together.

   I've hidden the background layer in Figure 3.27 in order to show you what areas I have erased. If it looks smooth in Photoshop, it will look good tiled across geometry.

6. Flatten the image and repeat the same process above for the top and bottom of the image. Ta-da! You have an artistically chosen seamless and tilable image (see Figure 3.28).

> **TIP**
>
> A quick and effective way to test how well your image is tiling is to make the bitmap your desktop wallpaper and set it to tile. You'll quickly be able to see whether it's working for you or not.

3.27 Erase the majority of the layer, leaving the edges.

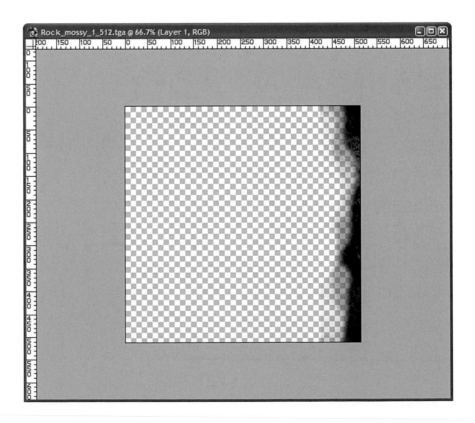

Another option I have found to be effective when artistic touch is not as necessary is to use Adobe ImageReady. There is a filter called Tile Maker (Filter>Other>Tile Maker) that does a nice job, although it can sacrifice resolution by cropping too much. I usually start with the following options in Tile Maker: Blend Edges Mode, Width set to 10 percent, and Resize Tile to Fill Image checked. Adjust the percentage until you get the tile you are looking for.

ACTIONS

Actions in Photoshop can be a very valuable tool for making exact changes to multiple images. I found that actions was my best friend when working on shell art. (The shell is the user interface art in a video game.) For *Medal of Honor*™, we had over 600 images making up the user interface. When I realized that we were going to have to desaturate all of these images by 50%, I was looking at another all-nighter!

Thanks to Photoshop's Actions, the job only took a few minutes. Actions have unlimited uses; you just have to be creative and keep them in mind when you get in a bind.

Let's see how Actions work by working through an example.

1. Open the four images called shapes 1-4 in Photoshop (see Figure 3.29).

   Imagine that these are a sequence of images used in the interface of your game. (We'll use only four images for this example, but

3.29 A sequence of interface images.

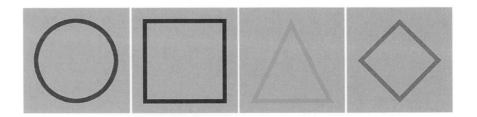

try to envision 50 images.) Your art director comes up to you and asks you to make some changes to the color, brightness, and saturation of all the bitmaps. Now, we could change one of the images, and write down every step and value we used to achieve that result, and repeat it one by one on each of the bitmaps. Or we can use actions.

2. Start by making sure that your Actions window is open in Photoshop. Go to Window>Actions and be sure it is checked. At the bottom of the Actions tab, click the New Action button, which is a small button at the bottom that looks exactly like the Create New Layer button in your Layers window.

   Name the action Color_tweak_1 or something similar. Photoshop is now recording what you are doing to the image until you say it's through. Adjust the brightness/contrast, then the saturation, and finally the color balance. Hit the Stop button.

3. Now select one of the other images and hit Play. You'll see the same value changes take place on the second image! You can also do large batch processing by going to File>Batch. Here you can choose any action, select to and from folders, and even change and append filenames so you don't overwrite your originals.

3.30 The Action window.

CONCLUSION

Taking the extra time to put some creative thought and effort into textures is what will help you stand out as an artist. Remember the philosophy of always improving on what you do, and continue to do your best to raise the bar with all your work. You'll find this same idea resonates throughout this book and applies in particular to Chapter 2, "Modeling Theory."

4

ADVANCED TEXTURING

A S I'M SURE YOU HAVE GATHERED by now, texturing plays an incredibly significant role in games. Relying on texture to compensate for the lack of detailed geometry and the responsibility of painting the world the players will see becomes extremely important. There is a reason why this chapter appears before the advanced modeling chapter: It's because I feel it's very important to be thinking about your work as a whole, not just in compartmentalized roles like texturing or modeling or lighting. Understanding some of the methods and tricks you can use to take full advantage of texture is important to think about before you start to create complex models. Why take the time and use up the memory to model a detail if you can add it effectively in texture? This chapter will focus on some of the useful ideas and processes I have found to be exceedingly valuable for texturing in games. Chapter 5, "Applying Textures," will address the details and specifics of actually applying textures to your geometry. Up until now, we've discussed the importance of creating the history and story behind your textures. This chapter will focus more on the artistic choices you can make when creating textures that exceed expectations and take your scene to the next level.

I preached extensively in the last chapter about the importance of telling the story behind the object and taking that extra time to make it something special. Now let's take a look at some of the actual tools and methods you can use to create that history. We'll start by exploring some essential features and workflows in Photoshop.

We've talked about Photoshop being an extremely powerful and useful piece of software. In this chapter, we'll focus more on the process and workflow of using Photoshop to its fullest potential. We're also going to look at some of the tools that I find I use most when painting textures. Keep in mind, as with nearly everything we discuss in this book, there is no absolute *right* way to do something. What really matters is how your texture comes out in the end. But process is important. We'll discuss some shortcuts and effective methods of working that I have developed and learned over the years, but I'm hoping you will take the initiative to come up with your own solutions and ideas.

THE POWER OF LAYERS

The heart of Photoshop, and what makes it such an incredible and versatile program, is its use of layers. By working with layers, you have an unlimited amount of control over your images. There seems to be nothing you can't accomplish in Photoshop, and it's because of the power of layers.

Again, I assume that you already have an understanding of layers and how they work. But just in case you need a quick refresher, think of layers as sheets of transparent cellophane paper that you can stack on top of one another. You can paint whatever you want on each individual sheet, but the image as a whole is what you see when all the sheets are combined.

One of the most important lessons I learned early on was not to be afraid to have tons of layers in my images. It is not uncommon to have up to 20 layers in a PSD (Photoshop Document) file. In fact, I sometimes work with images that have 50-plus layers! The only downsides to having so many layers are that your PSD file will be large and, depending on the amount of RAM you have on your computer, it could potentially cause problems. In addition, too many layers can get confusing to work with if you don't label and link them properly. However, PSD files tend to be *working* files that are not typically used as textures, so file size is not really an issue (unless you have a computer with less than 100MB of hard drive space!).

The clearest advantage to having multiple layers is that you can have individual control over the elements in your image. The same concept is used in compositing for postproduction of feature films. Each element that can be separated out from the background is kept on its own layer. That way, if four different explosions are being composited on top of the footage, it's very easy to tweak each individual explosion and not worry about affecting the entire scene. This also prevents the need to re-render the entire scene and all the elements along with it. Each element can be color corrected, transparency adjusted, or transformed without affecting the rest of the image.

The same advantages hold true for you when working in layers in Photoshop. Of course, you need to be smart and not go to the extreme unless you need to. If you have a metal plate with 200 rivets around the border, do you really need each rivet to be on its own layer? Probably not. But in situations where you have major features that you know you might want to tweak once you see them in the game, keep them on their own layers. If you don't give yourself the control that layers provide, you might end up kicking yourself later for not doing so.

Using layers along with the hide and show options (the eyeballs to the left of each layer) in Photoshop also lets you keep multiple versions of a texture all in one file. Let's say you created a painted wood texture for your scene. Without much effort at all, it's easy to duplicate the original layer and change its color. Do this a few times, and now you have several versions of the texture that you can show to your art director or quickly test in the game. Figure 4.1 is a good example of this technique.

4.1 Using layers to store multiple images in one file.

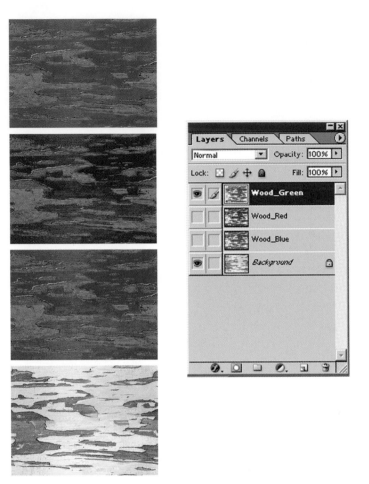

Another advantage to using multiple layers, and a more artistic one, is blending and adding depth. It's rare for the layers I create to be 100% opaque. Using transparency on layers enables you to subtly blend elements, which results in a more cohesive and textured image. Whether I'm creating metal, wood, stucco, or nearly any textured surface, I frequently use many layers with varying opacities to get the right look. Layering textures on top of one another also gives the image more depth, and ultimately makes it more interesting to look at. Blending textures is also a fast way to add detail. If you took the time to hand paint all these changes, you'd have your hands full. In Figure 4.2 I've started with a basic metal texture. By adding and mixing layers, I can capture certain features of each metal and blend them to get the exact look I'm going for.

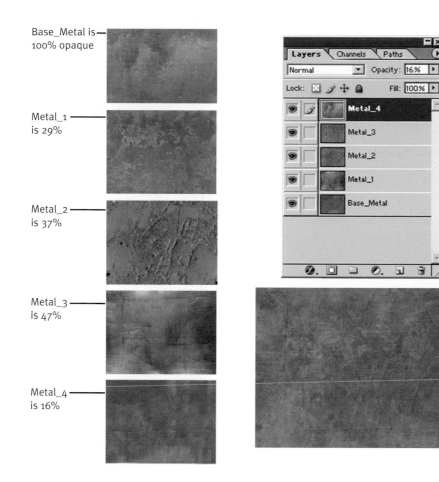

Base_Metal is 100% opaque

Metal_1 is 29%

Metal_2 is 37%

Metal_3 is 47%

Metal_4 is 16%

4.2 Using layers and opacity (transparency) to give textures more depth and character.

This method also gives you realistic texture because you are combining elements of real images and photographs, capturing the details and subtleties that are tough to create on your own. You'll find that the more layers you have, the more deep and complex the image becomes.

CREATING LAYERS

There are several ways to create new layers in Photoshop. Here are a few common methods.

First, you can go to the Layer menu, and choose Layer>New>Layer. You can do the same thing using the Layers palette, which is in the lower-right corner of the screen. At the bottom of the Layers palette is a small icon that looks exactly like the New Action icon we discussed in the previous chapter. Figure 4.3 shows the Create New Layer icon. Also, whenever you copy and paste an element, a new layer will be created that contains that new element.

The opacity of each layer can be controlled in the upper-right corner of the Layers palette. Opacity is shown in Figure 4.4.

In addition to being able to control the opacity of layers, each layer can be composited or blended with dozens of modes. To the left of the Opacity setting in the Layers palette is a field that says Normal. If you open that pull-down menu you'll see all the modes that Photoshop can use to blend your layers (Figure 4.5). Multiply, Lighten, Darken, and Luminosity are a few of the blend modes that I use most. Try them out and see how each one changes your image.

We'll talk about layers more as we move through the chapter. Now let's talk about some of the most often used features in Photoshop for painting textures.

The Create New Layer icon

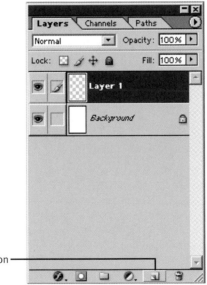

4.3 The Create New Layer icon in the Layers palette.

4.4 Each layer has its own opacity.

Opacity setting

PHOTOSHOP TOOLS

Of the billions of tools and features available in Photoshop, I find that I use several consistently, and rely on them heavily to create textures. I'll break them down into menus and point out the tools I use most. I encourage you to try all the tools in Photoshop as you work. The best way to learn is to experiment.

IMAGE MENU

The Image menu gives you control over how the existing image appears. Keep in mind that the majority of the tools in this menu affect the entire image, as opposed to individual layers. Some of the most commonly used commands under this menu are briefly covered here:

■ Mode Menu (Image>Mode)—I pointed out the Mode options in the previous chapter. Mode lets you change whether the image is RGB, CMYK, Indexed Color, and so on (see Figure 4.6).

■ Image Size (Image>Image Size)—I discussed Image Size (see Figure 4.7) in the previous chapter. It is available from the Image menu or by right-clicking on the top bar of the image itself. As you texture for games, you'll find yourself using this option time and time again.

■ Rotate Canvas (Image>Rotate Canvas)—This one is pretty self-explanatory. Use this tool to flip or rotate your image. Figure 4.8 shows the Rotate Canvas menu.

■ Image Adjustments (Image>Adjustments)—The Adjustments are powerful and useful tools for tweaking and perfecting your image. The commands that fall under this menu are some of the most repeatedly used ones in Photoshop:

■ Brightness/Contrast (Image>Adjustments>Brightness/Contrast)—This is one of my favorite commands. I constantly adjust the Brightness and Contrast of layers, channels, and entire images. It's a great tool for quickly tweaking your image and perfecting the look you are going for. Use it to balance the darks and lights of your image (see Figure 4.9).

■ Color Balance (Image>Adjustments>Color Balance)—This is a great tool for carefully controlling the color in your image. As opposed to changing the overall hue of the entire image, Color Balance lets you choose shadows, midtones, or highlights and subtly change the colors. It also is a great way to quickly add color to a desaturated image (see Figure 4.10).

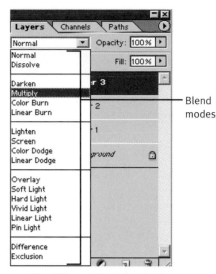

4.5 The different blend modes in Photoshop.

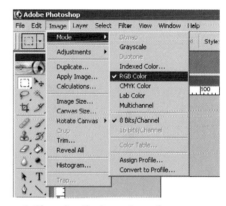

4.6 Changing the image's mode.

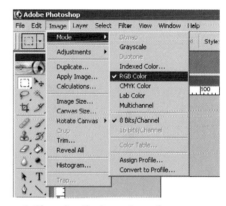

4.7 Changing image size.

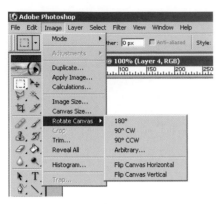

4.8 Image>Rotate Canvas.

4.9 Brightness/Contrast is one of the most frequently used tools in Photoshop.

4.10 Color Balance.

4.11 Hue/Saturation.

■ Hue/Saturation (Image>Adjustments>Hue/Saturation)—A very powerful and useful command, Hue/Saturation lets you quickly change the existing colors (their hues) and accentuate or reduce the amount of saturation (see Figure 4.11). I use this most often to selectively bring down the saturation of an image when it is too blown out in the game.

LAYER MENU

The Layer menu offers specific controls over individual layers, making it one of the more impressive and useful menus in Photoshop. Here are some of the highlights:

■ Adjustment Layers (Layer>New Adjustment Layer)—Imagine you have 25 layers in a file and you want to see what a Brightness/ Contrast change would look like on the whole image. Well, you could tweak the Brightness/Contrast for each of the 25 layers individually, which might take some serious time. Another option would be to flatten the image, then adjust the Brightness/Contrast. But then you lose your layers. This is where adjustment layers come into play. You can keep your 25 layers and create a new Brightness/ Contrast adjustment layer that sits above all the other layers in the Layers palette. By default, it will affect each layer below it, and it can be tweaked anytime. You can also link an adjustment layer to specific layers only. The types of adjustment layers you can create are the same as those in the Image>Adjustments menu. This tool is easy to use and a great time saver. Think about the Image>Adjustments tools we discussed in the previous section—you can create adjustment layers for any of those and retain completely independent control! Figure 4.12 shows the New Adjustment Layer menu.

LAYER STYLES

Some of my favorite and most frequently used features reside in this menu. Essentially, the features are effects that can be added to your layers to give them some extra punch. (In fact, in older versions of Photoshop, this menu was called Layer Effects.)

■ Drop Shadow (Layer>Layer Style>Drop Shadow)—As much as I want to say, "EVERYTHING looks better with a drop shadow!," I'm aware of many situations where that statement would be proven quite wrong. Drop shadows (see Figure 4.13), even in the subtlest example, add depth and tie elements to the image. I highly suggest experimenting with the Drop Shadow feature to see what it can do to accentuate your elements. But, before you go shadow crazy, think carefully about the context of your texture. If you are 100% sure of where that texture will appear in the game and are 100% positive about where your light source will be, adding a drop shadow with the correct light angle will allow you to add details and simulate geometry very effectively. But if you add a shadow, and it contradicts the light source in your scene, it will appear awkward and unnatural when viewed by the player.

- Outer Glow (Layer>Layer Style>Outer Glow)—Another series of effects that helps tie elements to the images and can create a sense of depth are glows (see Figure 4.14). Glows, whether they be outer or inner, have many uses. They can be very effective for simulating small light glows in a texture. For example, let's say you have a computer panel with various lights. You could use Outer Glow to convince the eye that the light is illuminating the surrounding area.

- Bevel and Emboss (Layer>Layer Style>Bevel and Emboss)—Like Drop Shadow, Bevel and Emboss is a very useful tool for game artists because it enables you to create the illusion of three-dimensionality in a texture (see Figure 4.15). But the same rules apply: Be sure you know your light source and direction, or it will do more harm than good. Bevel and Emboss lets you choose a light direction and, by using highlighted and darkened areas, creates the impression that an element is popping off the image and has depth. As I'm sure you can imagine, there are endless situations in game texturing where this can be useful—everything from rivets to detailed surface features like wiring, veins, or emblems.

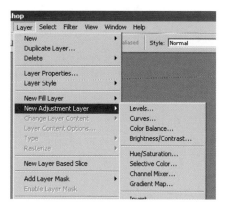

4.12 New Adjustment Layer menu.

4.13 Drop Shadow.

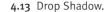

4.14 Outer Glow.

4.15 Bevel and Emboss.

FILTERS

Most anyone who has used Photoshop will tell you that filters are one of the most characteristic and unique features of the software. I'm not going to spend too much of your time discussing filters because they tend to be the type of tools that require some exploration and experimentation. Each filter is unique, and I encourage you to try them all. That way, over time, you will get a clear idea of what to expect from each of them. I'll just point out a few that I have found most useful and effective:

■ Plastic Wrap (Filter>Artistic>Plastic Wrap)—I use Plastic Wrap to give certain objects a shiny or wet look. The filter essentially works like it sounds: It covers your image with what looks like plastic shrink wrap. It's great for making a surface look more specular or polished. In Figure 4.16, the image on the right shows the effect of Plastic Wrap.

■ Gaussian Blur (Filter>Blur>Gaussian Blur)—Photoshop has a few blur algorithms to choose from, but I find that Gaussian Blur gives me the most predictable and controllable results. Aside from the obvious applications of blurring, like motion blur or depth of field, I find that I use it to soften many textures that have too much contrast and cause aliasing problems, or are too sharp due to resizing. When high contrasts of darks and lights are too close to one another in a texture, you tend to get bad aliasing problems. Blur can help reduce that effect. Figure 4.17 shows a Gaussian Blur on the right.

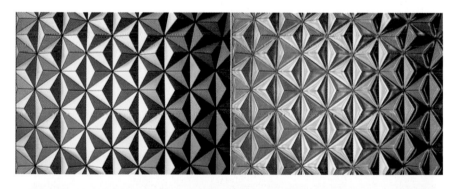

4.16 The Plastic Wrap filter applied to the image on the right.

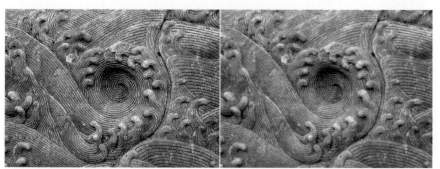

4.17 The Gaussian Blur filter applied to the figure on the right.

- Add Noise (Filter>Noise>Add Noise)—This is one of my most frequently used filters. One of the greatest advantages of adding noise is that you can take an image that is very clean and looks computer generated and add noise to get a more organic and realistic image. It's almost like adding an additional layer of grunge or dirt to your bitmap, giving it a more natural appearance. The left side of Figure 4.18 shows a simple, red square created in Photoshop; on the right is the same square with a Noise filter, which looks less computer generated.

- Sharpen (Filter>Sharpen>Sharpen)—Think of Sharpen as the opposite of Blur. It gives the image more crisp features and contrast. I use Sharpen when I have to take an image that is low resolution and increase it. Sharpen helps compensate for the loss of quality by refining the pixels in the image. I typically use a combination of Sharpen and Gaussian Blur to "rez-up" an image. In Figure 4.19, you can see the original, small texture on the left. It was resized, a Sharpen filter was applied to bring out the details and add pixels, and then it was subtly blurred again to soften the entire image.

- Craquelure (Filter>Texture>Craquelure)—This filter helps to give a surface more depth and organic appearance by adding a crackly, almost leather type of texture across the image. Keep in mind, this is not a filter to use to the extreme, but used sparingly and subtly, you'll find it can really help give your texture a more interesting look. Figure 4.20 shows before and after appearances using the Craquelure filter.

In addition to all the filters that come packaged with Photoshop, there are hundreds of third-party filters available for download. I highly suggest you take some time to try out those that sound interesting and see

4.18 The Add Noise filter can take away the computer-generated look.

4.19 "Rez-ing up" an image using Sharpen and Blur: the original small texture (left), the resized and sharpened texture (middle), and the texture blurred to soften the details (right).

4.20 The Craquelure filter adds more organic texture.

what they can do. Using an adjustment layer with filters gives you the ability to "fade" the texture immediately after application. Adjusting the opacity or blending mode of an applied filter can dramatically enhance the impact and realism. But keep in mind, even though filters can save you time, be careful not to rely on them too much. Your painting skills in Photoshop should take a front seat to any filters you might find.

ALPHA CHANNELS

I'm going to start off by saying that alpha channels are possibly the single most creatively flexible image component on the planet. And yet they have no color! There is so much you can do with simple grayscale information. From transparency to displacement maps, the uses for alpha channels are seemingly endless. Even though today's games are crawling with alpha channels that are being used for many different purposes, I believe they are still one of the most under-used tools we have as artists.

This section focuses on developing an understanding of what alpha channels are and how they can be used to make the most of your scene. We'll discuss different types of alpha, how to paint them, and how to bring them into your software. As you move through the rest of the book, you'll find that alpha channels will continue to play a big role in everything from texturing to modeling to user interface design. So pay close attention, and enjoy!

WHAT IS AN ALPHA CHANNEL?

An alpha channel is simply a grayscale image that is embedded in the extra 8 bits of a 32-bit image. As you undoubtedly already know, grayscale means black and white and anything in between. We've discussed the different file formats and pointed out that certain formats support an extra channel of information. TIF, TGA, PNG, and others support alpha channels. You'll also hear this type of image referred to as an RGBA image, meaning red, green, blue, and alpha. Let's take a look at the anatomy of a 32-bit image with an alpha channel. We'll use Red_circle.tga as a simple example (see Figure 4.21). This image is available from the book's page on the New Riders web site.

You'll notice that the image has only one layer (see Figure 4.22). When you click on the Channels tab in Photoshop's Layers palette (right next to the Layers tab) you'll see the RGB channels for the image (Figure 4.23).

The top channel is the RGB channel, showing us a composite of all three colors that make up the image, and giving us the final color. The

4.21 Red_circle.tga. A 32-bit image with the alpha channel shown on the right.

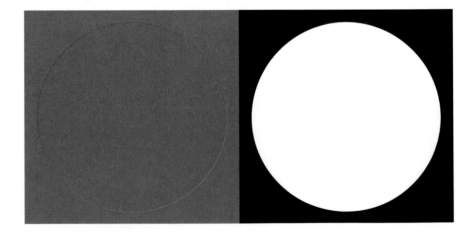

4.22 The bitmap needs only one layer.

channels below are each color on its own. Because this image is pure red, you'll notice that the Red channel is pure white, meaning that it has all the red it can possibly have in it, but the Green and Blue channels are black, meaning they are not contributing any color at all to the image. That's why we have a pure red color in the final image: Red is the only contributing color channel. To further clarify, a pure-white Red channel indicates that the channel contains 100% red. Likewise, a 20% gray fill in this channel would indicate 20% red.

Below the color channels, you'll see a fifth channel called Alpha 1. Here is our alpha information. This particular alpha channel uses strictly black and white, but an alpha can be composed of any value of grayscale. This additional alpha information is embedded in the image when it is saved, and can be used for a seemingly endless number of purposes.

4.23 The Channels tab reveals the individual channel information.

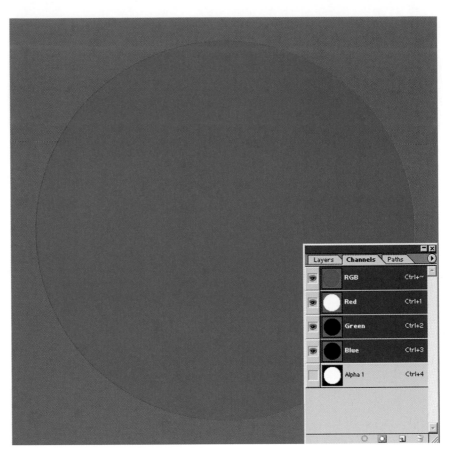

WHAT CAN ALPHA DO?

As I just mentioned, alpha channels have many uses, and are an extremely powerful tool for texturing. Some of the most common situations where alpha is used are:

- Transparency
- Bump maps
- Specularity
- Reflection
- Displacement
- Translucency
- Self-illumination (luminence)
- Light projection maps
- Masking

Let's take a look at a few of these that are most frequently used in games: transparency, bump maps, and specularity.

TRANSPARENCY

Games rely heavily on alpha transparency because of its ability to provide detail and effects that otherwise would cost a fortune in memory. You can use transparency to define everything from water to smoke to simulating detailed geometry. Let's use red_circle.tga as a continuing example.

Create a square plane in 3D, and assign the red_circle.tga texture to it. Even though we know there is an alpha channel embedded in the image, it will not be used by the 3D package unless we tell it to. Figure 4.24 shows what we initially see, which is only the RGB effects of the image, just like any other texture. But if we ask the software to use the alpha information for transparency, here is what we get (see Figure 4.25). So let's look at the relationship between that black-and-white information and the geometry we see in 3D.

The 3D software looks at the alpha information and determines that any part of the image that is white will be visible and opaque. Any part of the image that is black will be completely transparent. So what happens if the circle in the alpha channel is gray? You guessed it—semi-transparency (see Figure 4.26).

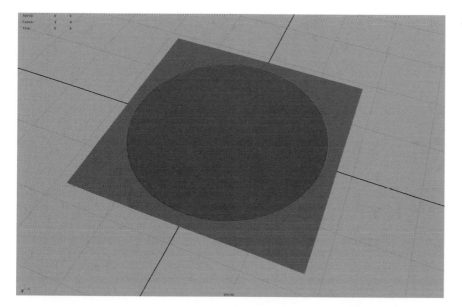

4.24 Red_circle.tga applied to a plane, not using the embedded alpha information.

4.25 Alpha transparency!

4.26 Using the full spectrum of grayscale, different levels of transparency can be achieved.

You can instantly see how this technique can apply to windows, water, or virtually anything transparent. Figure 4.27 shows how alpha transparency can be used for glass.

Look closely at the alpha channel (see Figure 4.28). You can see where I added the broken glass by simply making that area black and adding subtle white highlights on the edges to give it a 3D look. I also used varying shades of gray around the edges of the window frames to give the impression of dust and grunge. If you are going to use any alpha channel, be sure to use it!

4.27 A window texture using alpha transparency.

4.28 A window texture using alpha transparency.

Transparency is very cool, but why is this so important to games? Well, it comes back to being efficient. For the sake of simplicity, imagine you needed to make a red disk for use in a game. You could spend 200 polys to make a perfectly round disk out of geometry (see Figure 4.29).

On the other hand, you could use a simple alpha texture and a two-poly plane. Give that some thought and you'll start to see the potential advantages of using transparency to define geometry. I use alpha channels to define seemingly complex geometry that is small enough or far enough away that the player will not notice it is only two-dimensional. Figure 4.30 shows a lamp sconce that appears to be more complex than it really is. You'll also notice this technique used frequently in games for fences, gates, latticework, and similar objects.

4.29 A smooth disk made of polygons.

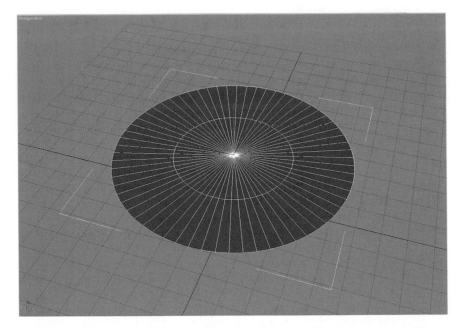

4.30 A lamp sconce where detail is added with alpha transparency instead of geometry.

Take a look at the images in Figure 4.31 from *Medal of Honor Frontline*™. See how many places you can spot that use alpha transparency. I think you'll be surprised.

4.31 See if you can spot all the areas where alpha transparency is being used.

I've marked some of the objects with red in Figure 4.32, but here are a few examples:

- The scaffold across the U-boat holding pen—all alpha
- The hanging power lines
- The glow around the light
- The shadow on the ground
- The railings and fences

4.32 Some of the objects are marked in red.

Medal of Honor Frontline™ IMAGES COURTESY OF ELECTRONIC ARTS INC. © 2002 ELECTRONIC ARTS INC. ALL RIGHTS RESERVED.

And don't forget the user interface elements like the compass and text in the upper corners. All use alpha transparency. I think you get the idea, but take a look at the train station and you'll see a few more examples.

Needless to say, alpha transparency is a powerful ally, and can help you make what may not be a very detailed scene look extremely detailed.

CHOOSE YOUR BACKGROUND COLOR CAREFULLY

An important point to remember when creating bitmaps for use as alpha transparency is your background color. For the examples I have shown you so far, I have intentionally made the background color different from the color of the elements in the image to demonstrate the idea more clearly. Most artists choose a black background for the areas that will be transparent. It's easier to visualize than other colors, and makes a clear distinction.

What many artists do not realize is that when the transparency is calculated, a row or two of pixels around the outer edge often get displayed. Despite your clear intentions in Photoshop, they can bleed over and display the background color of the image. When creating alpha images in this way, the pixels typically turn out to be a black border around the edge that can easily obliterate the effect you were trying to achieve. The solution is to try and match your background color to the edge color of the image. In the previous examples, I showed you the red circle with a gray background. Figure 4.33 shows the way it really should be to prevent pixel bleeding.

Next we'll discuss another common use for alpha channels in games—bump maps.

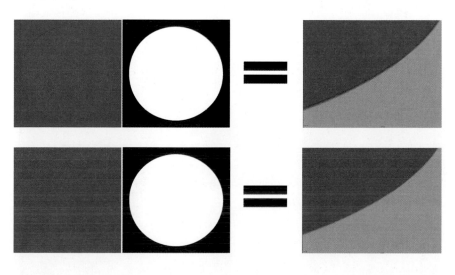

4.33 The background (the area that will be transparent) should be the same color as the edge of the image that will be opaque. Otherwise, you may get pixel bleeding.

BUMP MAPS

Many games are currently using bump maps to simulate more complex and detailed surfaces. Bump mapping uses normal or height map information to create the illusion that surfaces have varying heights. Take a look at Figure 4.34; although quite cliché, a brick wall is a good example of how bump mapping works.

You can see that the bump map is nothing but grayscale information used to define depth. The dark areas recede and the lighter areas stand out. It's as simple as that.

The way that traditional bump mapping works in 3D rendering is that the normals for *each pixel* are tweaked based on the grayscale bump map that the artist creates. Then the lighting is calculated with these tweaked normals, giving the illusion that the surface is bumpy and varying in height. Because games have a hard time calculating lighting on a per-pixel basis, game engines take a different approach to bump mapping that is still quite effective. The engine essentially looks at the bump map and, using multiple pass rendering, creates highlights and dark areas across the map to simulate bump mapping (see Figure 4.35).

4.34 A brick wall without (left) and with (right) a bump map.

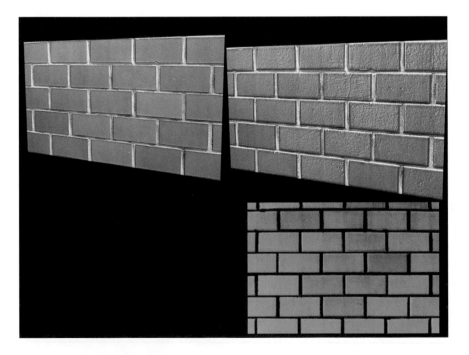

4.35 Bump mapping on the floor adds depth and realism (*Indiana Jones and the Emperor's Tomb* by LucasArts).

SPECULARITY MAPS (SPECULAR)

Another great use for alpha information is to define what areas of the model reflect light the most. A specular highlight is the area where light bounces off an object. Creating a specular map can give you even more control over the appearance of an object by suggesting that the surface qualities are not flat or uniform (see Figure 4.36).

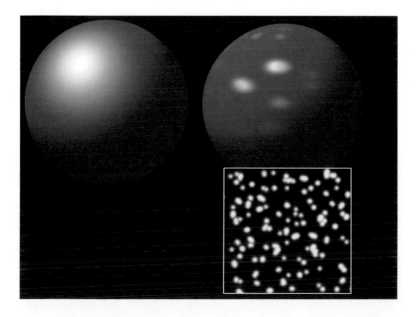

4.36 Using a specular map can give your surface a more interesting quality.

A very common use for specular maps is on a human face. We tend to be more oily or shiny on the bridge of the nose or forehead. A good specular map will accentuate these areas so light reflects more on them. Specular maps also work well for shiny metals, vehicles, and water. Providing that extra layer of information adds more depth to your model (see Figure 4.37).

4.37 A great use of specular on the water from *Knights of the Old Republic* by LucasArts.

HOW DO WE BRING THE ALPHA CHANNEL INTO THE 3D PACKAGE?

Now that you have your alpha information, let's talk about how to bring it into your 3D scene. We are going to discuss the texturing process in 3ds max and Maya more in the next chapter, but I want to offer you a frame of reference at this point. Each package is slightly different in how it handles alpha, but the rules are generally the same. Regardless of the package, your material or shader will have different channels for maps. The most obvious and commonly used channel is the Diffuse, or Color, channel. This is where your color bitmap (base texture) always goes. Let's look at the Material Editor in 3ds max (see Figure 4.38).

Now, depending on what you want to use your alpha channel for (bump, specular, displacement, and so on), choose a channel in the material and assign texture to the alpha. Let's use a bump map as a demonstration. Figure 4.39 shows the color texture in the Diffuse channel and the alpha in the Bump channel. This is how the software understands how you want to use that grayscale information.

> **NOTE**
>
> The small Diffuse box with an M in it is simply a shortcut to the diffuse channel below, because it is the most frequently used channel.

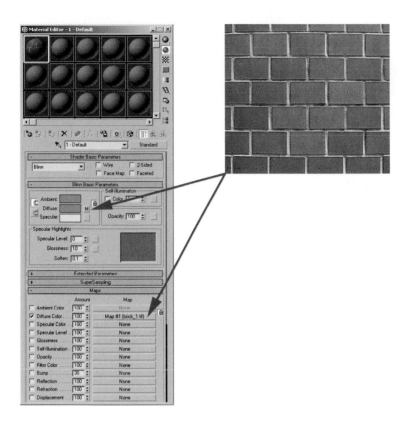

4.38 The Diffuse channel in 3ds max is where the base texture resides.

You typically have two options when bringing alpha information into 3D software. One option is to embed the alpha channel into the image, like we did in the previous example. The second option is to create an entirely separate grayscale bitmap to use as the alpha in addition to the original color bitmap. Hmmm…why do you think we embed the alpha when texturing for games? That's right: texture memory. One texture (even though it is 32-bit) is still cheaper than two textures. When you bring in a 32-bit alpha image, you would assign the same texture to both channels, and then tell the software to use the image's alpha channel for the bump map. There are advantages to keeping a separate alpha map, however, such as if you need to reuse an alpha channel with more than one texture in more than one place.

Let's next look at the same bump map setup in Maya's Hypershade (see Figure 4.40). Maya's Hypershade also has multiple channels that will take advantage of alpha information.

Just to solidify the point, let's think about the red circle image again. The alpha channel would actually go into the Transparency channel of the material. This is really quite simple (see Figure 4.41).

4.39 Placing the alpha texture in the Bump channel of the material lets the software know how you want to use your alpha.

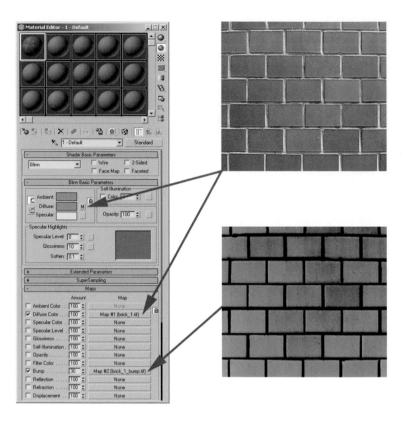

4.40 Setting up a bump map in Maya's Hypershade.

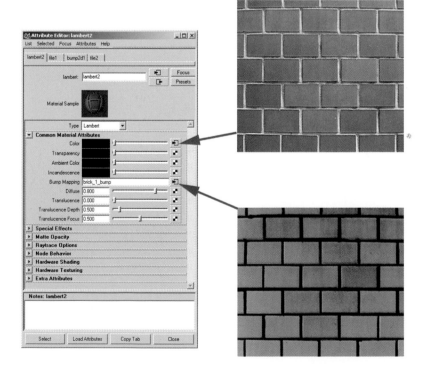

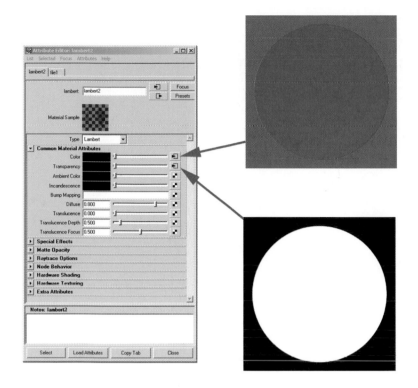

4.41 For alpha transparency, the grayscale goes into the Transparency channel of the material.

HOW TO MAKE ALPHA CHANNELS

Now that you have an idea of what alpha channels are and what they can do, let's discuss how to make them. There are dozens of ways to make an alpha channel, and just like anything else, there is no *right* way. You can paint the alpha channel by using the tools in Photoshop, use quick masks, or use any number of other methods. Again, all that matters is how it comes out in the end. Here are a couple of shortcuts I have learned to speed up the alpha channel process.

When I paint a new texture, especially one that I know is going to have an alpha channel, I of course always create new layers. One reason this is beneficial for alpha is that I can load the transparency of that layer and use it directly as an alpha channel. Let me explain. Let's use our trusty red circle again as an example. When I create the red circle, I make sure it is on a new layer (see Figure 4.42). (I'm keeping the background gray for clarity.)

Now I can load the selection of that layer to get my alpha selection. With the Marquee Selection tool, I right-click anywhere in the image and choose Load Selection (see Figure 4.43).

4.42 The red disk is on its own layer.

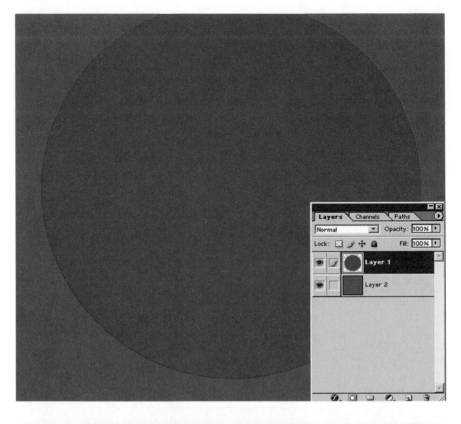

4.43 Load selection by right-clicking anywhere in the image.

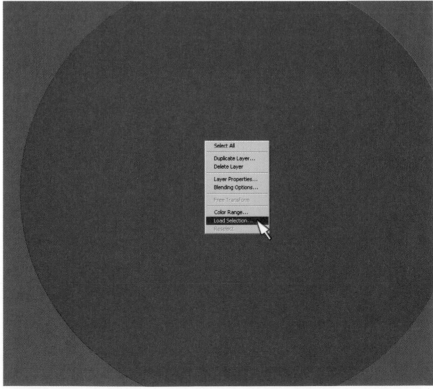

By default Photoshop assumes I want the transparency, and I do. Now the selection is perfectly snug around my circle (see Figure 4.44).

Now, while keeping the selection, click on the Channels tab in the Layers palette. Below the RGB channels, you'll see an icon that looks exactly like the Create New Layer icon. Click that, and a new alpha channel will appear (see Figure 4.45).

Next, all you have to do is use the Paint Bucket tool to fill your selection with white (or gray), and you have a perfect alpha channel (see Figure 4.46).

Instead of clicking on the Create New Channel icon to create a new alpha channel, you can make a selection and hit the Quick Mask mode icon in the toolbar (see Figure 4.47), and it will create a fast alpha channel for you. It will also automatically fill it with foreground color.

4.44 Use Load Selection to get the outline of the elements on that layer.

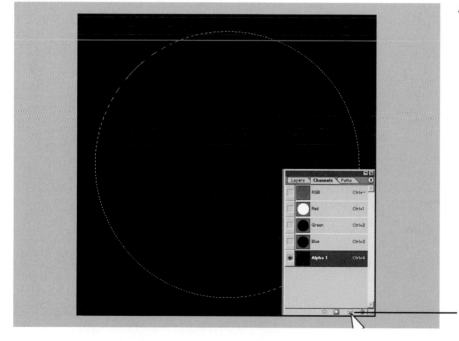

4.45 Click the Create New Channel icon. Photoshop assumes you want an alpha channel and names it appropriately.

The Create New Channel icon

4.46 Use the Paint Bucket tool to fill the selection.

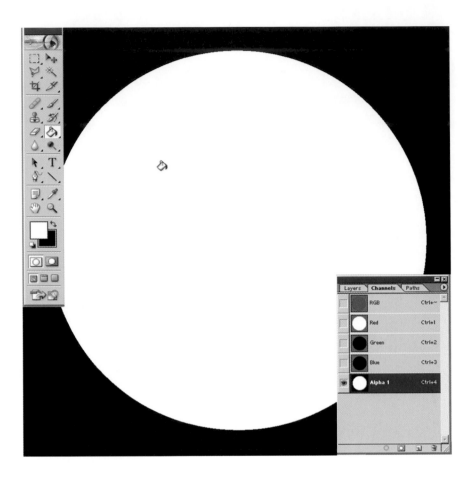

The Quick Mask mode icon.

4.47 The Quick Mask mode creates an alpha channel for you and fills it automatically.

SAVING THE FILE

The next important thing to remember after you create your alpha channel is how to save the image so that the information is embedded. To save a TGA (Targa) file with the alpha information, in Photoshop, choose Save As and choose Targa from the Format drop-down menu. When prompted, make sure the Alpha Channels box is checked (see Figure 4.48). Hit Save, and you will be prompted again for a bit depth. Choose 32 bits/pixel (see Figure 4.49). If you accidentally hit 24 or 16 bits/pixel, the image will not have an alpha channel embedded. It's a common mistake, and the first thing you should troubleshoot if alphas are not working.

As we have discussed before, Targa is not the only format that supports alpha channels. TIF format (as well as a few others like PNG and proprietary formats created by hardware manufacturers) also offer the additional channel for alpha.

4.48 Be sure to check the Alpha Channels box.

I typically name files that have an alpha channel with an "_A" at the end to remind me and others that it is a 32-bit image. All game companies and projects will have different naming conventions. It's just important to remember to name these files differently.

If you are Using Photoshop 7 and your alpha is not working for Targas, you'll need to go to the Adobe web site and update Photoshop to 7.1. It's free, and it fixes the problem. All other versions should be fine.

GAME ENGINES AND ALPHA

OK, so we know how to get the alpha into 3ds max or Maya, but how does it get into the game engine? Well, thank your friendly neighborhood programmer. Most game engines are set up to translate the choices you've made in the 3D software directly into the engine. If you have

4.49 Choosing 32 bits/pixel saves the additional 8 bits of alpha information in your image.

alpha transparency in Maya, the engine should know that you want to use that image's alpha for transparency. If you set it up for bump mapping, that should work as well.

However, it's not always that easy. With some engines you'll need to tag your textures so the engine knows what to do with them. An example might be naming a file something like Fence_1_TR.tga, where TR means transparency. Again, each project and engine is different, but agreeing on a solid naming convention is always beneficial.

CONCLUSION

We've seen what Photoshop is capable of, and how to create and use alpha channels. But that is only the tip of the iceberg. The purpose of this chapter was to give you an overview of how and why we use these types of textures in games. You'll find that the ideas established here are going to be elaborated on and revisited throughout the rest of the book. In Chapter 10, "Tips and Tricks," we'll explore tips and tricks that you can use to paint and assemble more sophisticated and complex textures. By now you should have a very clear idea of how games are theoretically put together and the responsibilities of the game artist. The rest of the book will take that knowledge to the next level and offer you an edge. Next, let's talk about how we apply these beautiful textures to our geometry.

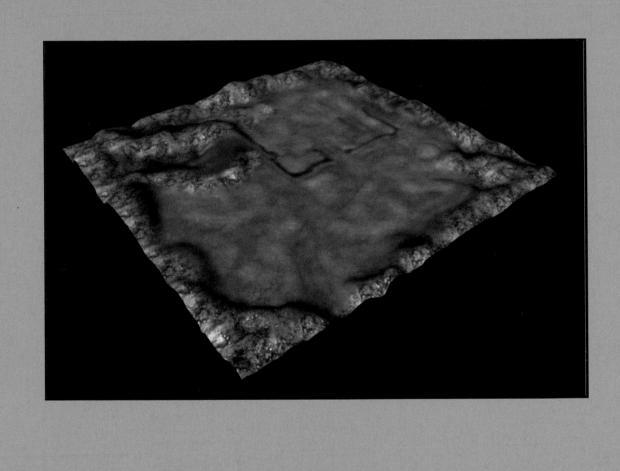

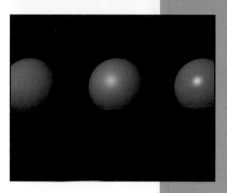

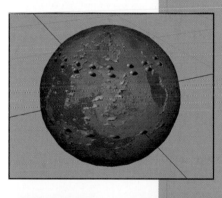

[**CHAPTER**]

5

APPLYING TEXTURES

N ow that you know the process for creating realistic and efficient textures, it's time to discuss how they are best applied to your models. Each type of geometry—NURBS, SUB-D, and polygons—follows a different approach when it comes to applying textures. When texturing with polygons for games, we use a method called UV mapping, which is the process of wrapping or projecting your texture onto your model. Many artists agree that texturing polygons can be one of the more time-consuming aspects of game art. Hopefully the explanations and methods established in this chapter will help you develop a clear understanding of the texturing process and enable you to bring together the models and textures you create in an effective and creative way. Before we get too involved with the specifics of UVs, I'd like to offer a quick refresher course on assigning materials in both 3ds max and Maya. For those of you who are familiar with the process, feel free to skip ahead.

ASSIGNING MATERIALS

Remember that a material or shader is the vessel that carries your actual bitmap texture. The material provides the surface quality, reflectivity, and so on. But the texture is what really gives your model its appearance. Let's take a look at how a material and texture are assigned to a model. Then we'll move on to the process of choosing

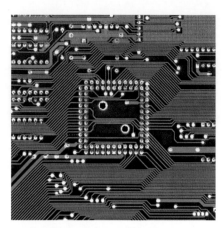

5.1 For this exercise, we'll assign Circuit.tga to a basic plane.

TIP

You can also create a new material by right-clicking anywhere in the window. You will get the same menu options this way, and it tends to speed up your workflow.

5.2 Maya's Hypershade.

how and where that texture appears. To keep things simple, our goal will be to assign a circuitry texture to a simple plane. Figure 5.1 shows the circuitry texture we want to assign.

MAYA'S HYPERSHADE

Each 3D package has its own way of organizing and applying materials. In Maya, it's called the Hypershade (Window>Rendering Editors> Hypershade). Figure 5.2 shows Maya's Hypershade.

The Hypershade is unique because not only does it display all the materials in your scene, but it also gives you access to lights, utilities, cameras, and even a project window that lets you browse files. As you texture polygons, you'll find you tend to stay focused on the material window, which gives you the control you need to assign and manage all the materials in your scene. When starting a new scene, the Hypershade always starts with a default material called lambert1. This is the basic material that is automatically assigned to any new object you create. So, to keep things simple, I always leave that default material alone. Figure 5.2 not only shows the Hypershade, but also shows the default lambert1 material.

To create a new material in Maya, go to the Hypershade's Create menu and select Create>Materials>Lambert. A new Lambert material will appear in the window (see Figure 5.3).

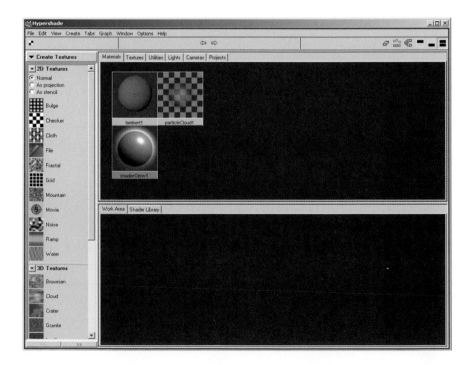

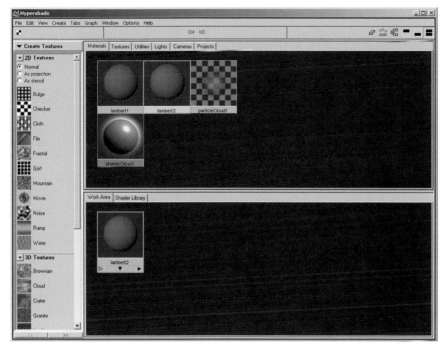

5.3 The new Lambert material.

I want to talk briefly about material types before we move forward. As you might notice, there are many different options when creating a new material—Lambert, Blinn, Phong, and so on. Each material type has its own qualities; for example, a Lambert material is flat type with no highlights or reflectivity. A Phong material has sharp, tight highlights and is typically a good material for highly reflective surfaces such as chrome. Blinn is a happy medium between the two; it has highlights and a semishiny surface, but in a way that is more subtle than a Phong. Most 3D packages offer these same material types.

Today's games, however, typically do not use material types. When we need to define surface characteristics, we rely on texture and alpha information to suggest specularity, bump, and the like, as opposed to translating that material information into the game engine. I can guarantee it will not always be that way. I'm sure that using material types like Phong and Blinn will become more commonplace in the not too distant future. But for now, we typically stick to Lambert materials to carry our bitmap textures because most game engines do not carry over the material's parametric attributes, only references to bitmaps. Despite the fact that these types are not taken advantage of as of yet, I highly recommend that you take some time to explore the different types and learn about their individual advantages and characteristics. Examples of three different material types are shown in Figure 5.4.

5.4 Maya's Hypershade material types. From left to right: Lambert, Blinn, and Phong.

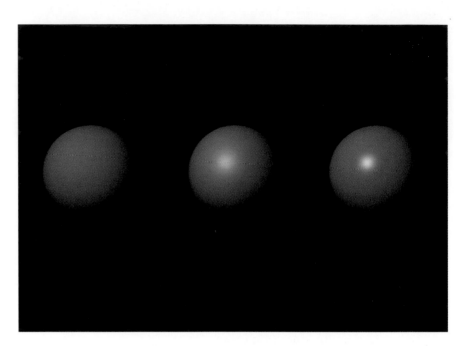

Once we have created a new material, we need to associate our circuit texture to the material. In the Hypershade, when you double-click the material, the Attribute Editor will open and expose the material's parameters. Whenever we choose a texture, we add it to the Color channel, which is the first channel in the Attributes list. Figure 5.5 shows the Attribute Editor and the Color channel in Maya.

If you click on the small, checkered box to the right of the word *Color*, you get a window asking you what type of texture you would like to place in this channel (see Figure 5.6). There are obviously many choices here, but the one we want is File, which means we have a bitmap we want to use as the texture.

When you click the File button, the Attribute Editor moves to a new input, asking you which bitmap you would like to use. We can browse to the file Circuit.tga by clicking the folder button (see Figure 5.7).

When you choose your texture, the Hypershade will update and you'll see that the material now has the Circuit.tga texture assigned to it. As shown in Figure 5.8, the texture is now part of the material. Now you have a material that is ready to be applied to geometry.

5.5 The attributes of a Lambert material. The Color channel is where we will assign the circuit bitmap we have created.

The Color channel

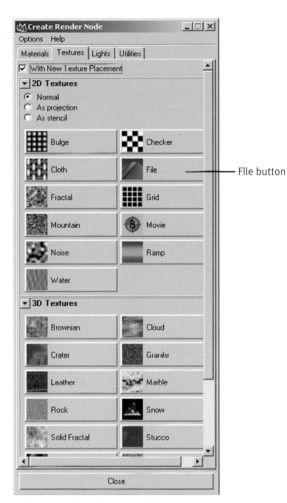

Flle button

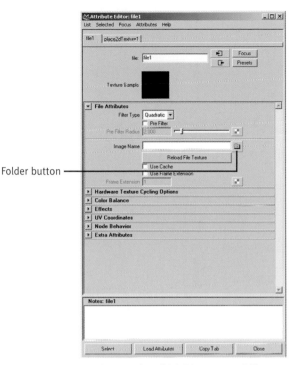

Folder button

5.7 Maya asks which bitmap you'd like to apply to the material.

5.6 Maya asks what type of texture you would like to place in the color channel.

We'll use a simple plane as the model we want to assign this texture to. Figure 5.9 displays the simple plane we want to assign the texture to.

With the plane selected, all you need to do is right-click on the material in the Hypershade and select Assign Material to Selection. The texture will now appear on the model (see Figure 5.10).

5.8 Circuit.tga is now the material's texture.

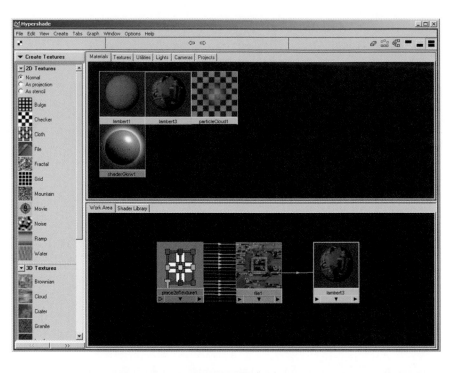

5.9 The plane is the geometry to which we want to assign the texture.

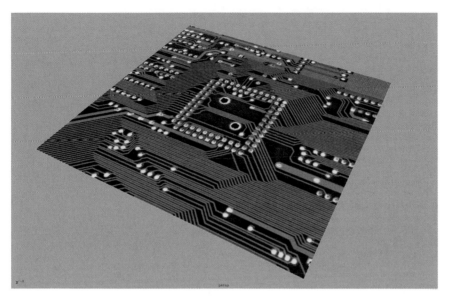

5.10 The plane now has circuit.tga assigned to it.

Pretty straightforward. Now let's take a look at the same process in 3ds max.

3DS MAX MATERIAL EDITOR

In 3ds max, we use the Material Editor to manage materials and textures (see Figure 5.11). You'll notice a lot of similarities between 3ds max and Maya when it comes to texturing. The basic ideas are the same. A pull-down menu lets you choose whether your material is a Blinn, Phong, and so on. You have various channels within the material to which you assign textures for Diffuse Color, Bump, Transparency, and the like. The Material Editor in 3ds max tends to be a bit more focused than Maya's Hypershade, however, because it is designed to manage only materials. Therefore, it offers some shortcuts and advantages that can speed up the texturing workflow.

In order to see all the different map channels, you need to expand the Maps rollout toward the bottom of the editor (see Figure 5.12). The channel that we are going to use to assign a texture is the Diffuse Color channel. This is essentially the same as the Color channel in Maya. As I mentioned in the previous chapter, there is a shortcut to the Diffuse Color channel at the top of the Editor (see Figure 5.13).

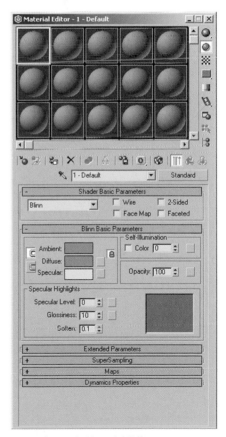

5.11 3ds max's Material Editor.

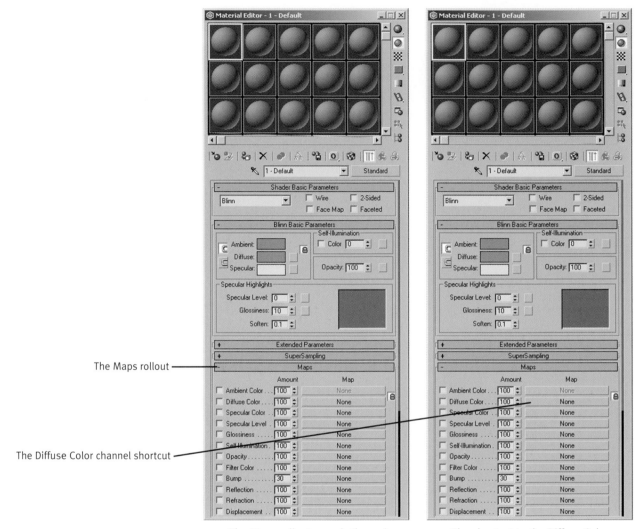

The Maps rollout

The Diffuse Color channel shortcut

5.12 The Maps rollout reveals the various channels available.

5.13 The shortcut to the Diffuse Color channel.

Click the Diffuse Color shortcut, and you'll see the Material Browser pop-up that serves the same function as the window in Maya. This window is asking you what type of texture you want to assign to the Diffuse Color channel. In this case, we want to choose Bitmap (see Figure 5.14).

You'll immediately be presented with a window where you can browse for the texture you want. We'll choose Circuit.tga again (see Figure 5.15).

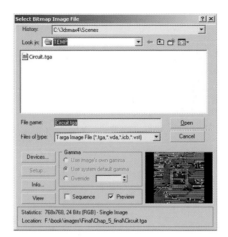

5.15 Browsing for Circuit.tga.

5.14 Choose Bitmap as your texture type.

When you select the bitmap, you'll notice that the material now has the texture associated with it. In order to now assign the material to the geometry, we need to go to the top of the materials hierarchy. To do this, just click the Go to Parent button, and you'll be back where you started (see Figure 5.16).

Now, with the geometry selected, all we have to do is hit the Assign Material to Selection button at the top of the editor (Figure 5.17).

Although we'd expect to see the texture appear on the plane now, we must complete one more step before it actually shows up in the viewport. To the far right of the Assign Material to Selection button, you'll see a blue and white checkered box (see Figure 5.18). This button is the Show Map in Viewport button. Click this, and we have a textured model (see Figure 5.19)!

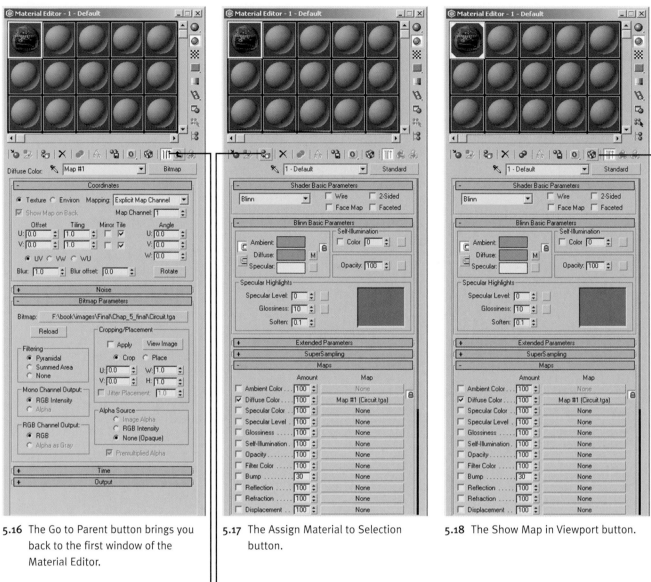

5.16 The Go to Parent button brings you back to the first window of the Material Editor.

The Go to Parent button

5.17 The Assign Material to Selection button.

Assign Material to Selection button

5.18 The Show Map in Viewport button.

The Show Map in Viewport button

OK, now that we know how to assign a texture to a model, we need to understand how to control the way that texture is applied to the geometry. For the previous exercise, it is pretty straightforward to assign a simple 2D texture to a flat, square surface in 3D. But what do we do when the models get more complex and we need precise control over how that texture wraps around the model? We start by understanding UV coordinates.

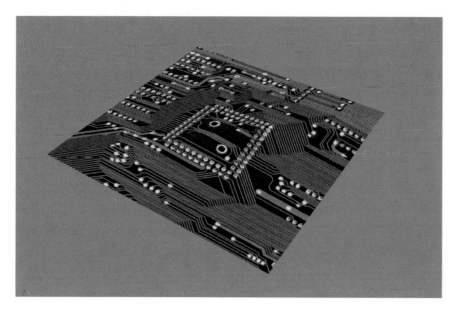

5.19 The textured plane in 3ds max.

WHAT ARE UVS?

When you apply a texture to geometry, you are wrapping a 2D image around a 3D model. UVs are the coordinates used to tell the computer where to place the texture in 3D space by taking each point of the model (vertex) and assigning it to a point on the map. Just like the X,Y, and Z coordinates, U and V are simply points of reference to tell us where something is in space. In the case of textures, it's called Texture Space, and it uses a 0 to 1 range to define space. Take a look at how texture space is set up in Figure 5.20. The grayed out area is the typical 0 to 1 texture space.

You can see that just like X,Y, and Z coordinates, the 0 to 1 texture space also has positive and negative values. So if you gave a vertex a UV coordinate of .5,.5 it would appear in the texture space as shown in Figure 5.21.

> **NOTE**
>
> Some packages like 3ds max offer a third coordinate (W) to give you the opportunity to flip the texture on the geometry. Don't let that concept confuse you; it's simply an added feature that can be achieved in any package using other methods.

5.20 Texture space and the UV coordinate system.

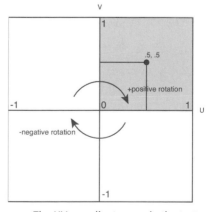

5.21 The UV coordinate .5,.5 in the texture space.

Most 3D packages automatically create and assign UV coordinates to the primitive objects you create. For example, when we created the simple plane in the last example, it already had default UV coordinates. That's why we could see the texture. This is a nice way to start because it lets you assign a texture and be able to see it on your object. Without UVs, the software does not know how to apply a texture, so it just won't show up. Even though primitive objects start off with default UVs, you'll almost always need to reassign new UVs or rearrange the existing UVs in order to get the desired result. To create a UV mapping arrangement that works best for your model, you may need to map it several times, using various types of projections, until you find a mapping arrangement that works well. If all you need is a simple cube, then the default UVs may work just fine for you. But as soon as you start to create more complex models, it's guaranteed you'll be creating new UV coordinates for your geometry.

PROJECTION MAPPING

One of the most common and useful ways to assign UV coordinates is to use a projection. A texture projection essentially takes the bitmap and projects it onto your geometry in a variety of ways. You'll find that the majority of the time, you'll be using one of these methods to give your objects UV coordinates. Take the time to learn how each type behaves. By default, most 3D packages have the same types of projection. Here are a few, along with brief explanations:

- Planar mapping—Probably the most common projection type, it's simple, predictable, and easy to understand. Imagine a film projector shining your texture onto a box. This is the type of projection we would have used if we needed to apply a vintage poster texture to the plane in the previous example. When you select geometry or a face and apply a planar projection, you are essentially giving that face perfect 0 to 1 UV coordinates. Figure 5.22 shows the poster example.

- Box (or Cubical) mapping—Box mapping is just like planar mapping, except that it projects planar maps on six sides in the shape of a cube based on the direction of the face normals. Obviously perfectly suited for cube-shaped objects, it is exemplified in Figure 5.23.

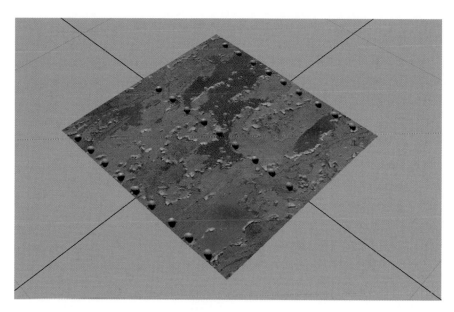

5.22 The poster texture projected on a plane.

5.23 Box mapping.

■ Cylindrical mapping—A cylindrical projection is not quite as easy to envision as a planar, but the way it works is also quite simple. The cylindrical projection is really a planar map that is wrapped around in a cylindrical shape. Obviously, the most appropriate use of this projection type is on geometry that is cylindrical in shape, such as tree trunks, bottles or cans, and pillars. Cylindrical maps are frequently used to generate UVs for the mapping of character faces. Figure 5.24 shows an example of cylindrical mapping.

5.24 Cylindrical mapping.

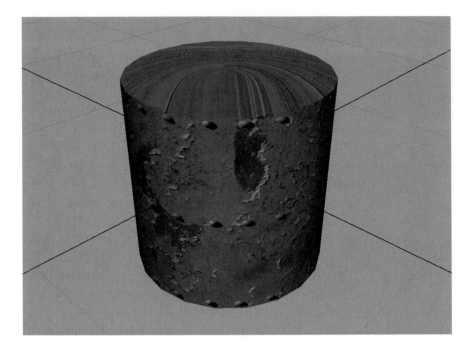

- Spherical mapping—Spherical mapping pinches the image at the top and bottom while stretching in the middle. Figure 5.25 shows the uniform checker texture applied with a spherical projection map. The texture will distort. Depending on the situation, this may or may not be desirable. You can easily correct this in Photoshop by using the Distort Filter (Filter>Distort>Spherize). Set the Mode to Vertical Only and the Amount to around −40. This will compensate for the distortion that takes place with a spherical mapped projection. I've used a checkerboard texture for this example to demonstrate more clearly. Figure 5.26 shows the effect of using the Spherize filter.

- Face mapping (called Unitize UVs in Maya)—Face mapping projects and fits the texture into the 0-to-1 texture space for every face on the model. Figure 5.27 shows a face-mapped sphere. I've added a red border to the checker texture so you can see what is happening more clearly.

All of these projections are fairly straightforward and easy to understand. The catch is, unless your geometry is a perfect cube, plane, cylinder, or sphere, you are bound to get some stretching and abnormalities. It works great for assigning UVs to simple objects, but once the models become more complex, you'll need more control over your UVs. That is where UV editing comes into play.

5.25 You can see how the texture distorts along the surface.

5.26 The checkerboard texture before and after the Spherize filter is applied.

5.27 Face mapping fits the texture into every face of the model.

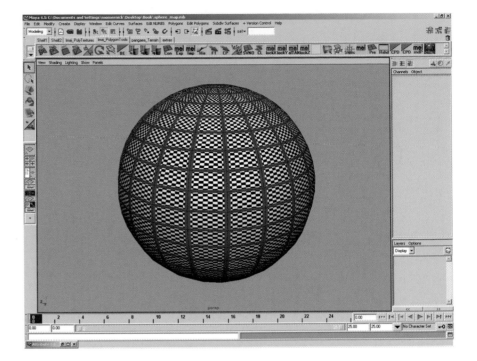

EDITING UVs

In addition to using a projection matrix to assign UV coordinates, each 3D package comes with the capability to manually edit your individual UVs to get the most precise and efficient coordinates.

Let's assume you have used one of the preceding methods to give your geometry UV coordinates. Now it's time to tweak and perfect them by manually adjusting your UVs. This is where texturing can become a bit tedious and time consuming. But, as you practice, you'll get faster and more efficient with assigning and adjusting these coordinates, so be patient and enjoy the process! Let's look at the options for Maya and 3ds max.

MAYA'S UV TEXTURE EDITOR

In Maya, you can access the UV Texture Editor by selecting a model or component and going to Window>UV Texture Editor. Figure 5.28 shows the UV Texture Editor window. It also shows the 3D geometry flattened out into a 2D image.

3DS MAX'S UV EDITING

To access 3ds max's UV editing capabilities, you need to go to the Modify tab and choose the Unwrap UVW modifier. Figure 5.29 shows you what you will get.

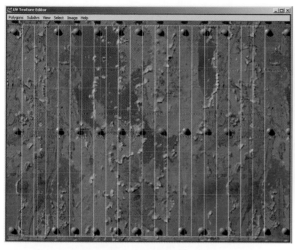

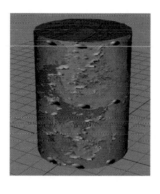

5.28 Maya's UV Texture Editor window allows you to manually control the individual UVs.

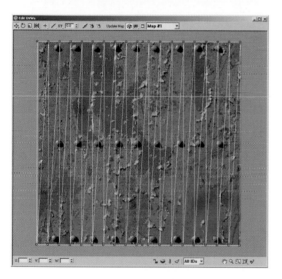

5.29 3ds max's Edit UVWs window.

COMPOSITE TEXTURES AND UVS

When choosing your texture sizes and quantities, you have many options. Game textures have historically been composite textures, which means that several textures are combined into one bitmap in order to load more quickly and take full advantage of texture space. You'll find a composite texture works very well for a complex model where you know elements of that texture will not be used elsewhere in the game. Texturing characters is a perfect example of the use of composite textures, due to the complexity of the models. Figure 5.30 shows a Stormtrooper and the composite texture that is assigned to him. Study the layout closely. The layout in Figure 5.30 should help you understand UVs more clearly.

5.30 A Stormtrooper and the composite texture.

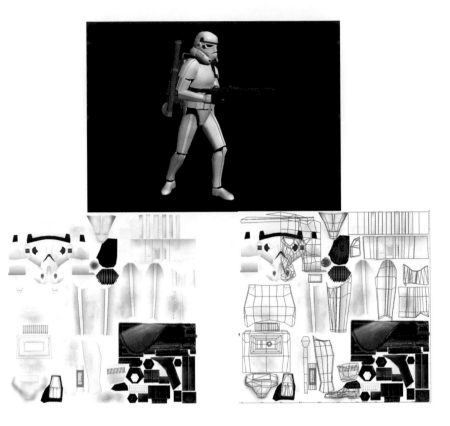

You can clearly see how each part of the model corresponds to a particular part of the map. Notice that even the weapon texture is part of the same map. This is a great example of efficient use of texture space—the use of UV coordinates at its best!

It's important to remember that just like with modeling or lighting, the more polygons you have on your model, the more accurate your UV editing can be. But, on the flip side, if you have too many polygons, you'll have such a jumbled mess of UVs, it could be nearly impossible to work with. So as with most everything, a healthy balance is needed.

ASSIGNING UVs

It's common for artists to choose a simple map like a checkerboard to first lay out their UVs, and then use that information to generate their texture when they are happy with the layout. As you gain experience and practice, you'll find that you can sometimes paint your texture and assign UVs afterwards. It really depends on the type of model you are texturing. Again, there is no absolutely correct way to apply UVs. The workflow changes depending on the model, and what really matters is how the texture looks in the end. Figure 5.31 shows two textures I sometimes use to get my UVs layed out before I start to paint the texture.

Having clearly labeled elements like Top, Bottom, Left, Right, or 1, 2, 3, 4 helps you keep your bearings when texturing. (You can download these images from the book's page on the New Riders web site: 1234.TGA and TBLR.TGA.)

Once you have your coordinates the way you like, you can start to create your final texture, and you'll know exactly where to paint.

Take some time to experiment with UVs and projections. It can be a time-consuming process, but as with anything else, practice makes perfect.

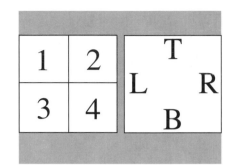

5.31 Two textures that work well for laying out your UVs.

MULTIPLE UV SETS

Maya, along with several other software packages, has a great feature that allows you to add an unlimited amount of UV coordinates for one model and assign different textures to each set of UVs. This is great for blending several textures or placing labels or stickers on existing textures. I have found it particularly useful for terrain. It allows you to seamlessly layer multiple textures on top of one another and associate each layer with an alpha channel that determines where that texture will show up. In addition, it's useful because you can tile the texture within the alpha mask to get more resolution. Of course, the more UV sets you have, the more expensive it will be. Take a look at Figures 5.32 and 5.33. You can see how several textures can work together to give the overall model more depth and realism. This is an efficient way to define roads and pathways.

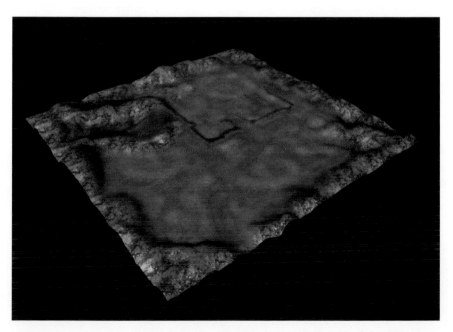

5.32 A terrain texture using multiple UV sets to blend several textures.

5.33 You can see how each texture is linked to an alpha mask. The corresponding texture will show up in the white areas of the alpha map.

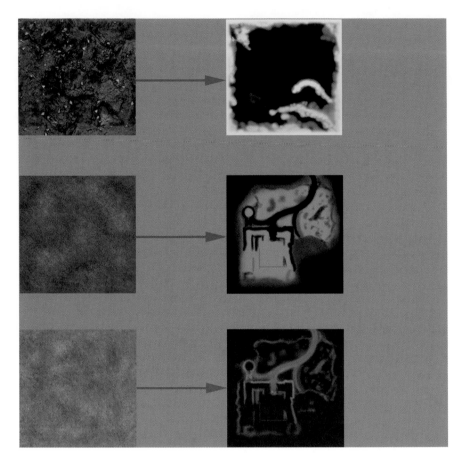

Even though this is only one piece of geometry, the complexity of texture gives it a strong sense of depth. You can see the relationships between the alpha channels and the individual textures. The alpha of the dirt layer in the base acts as a transparency mask that tells Maya where to allow the texture to show up. The grass is the next layer, and its alpha does the same. The rocky moss sits on top of them all, and reveals itself only where its alpha mask allows. And the beauty is that each texture can be tiled within its respective alpha mask.

To experiment with Maya's multiple UV sets, use a layered texture, which you can create in the Hypershade in combination with copying and pasting UV sets. This can be done using the Edit Polygons>Texture menu.

Now that we've discussed the concept of UVs, it's important to understand tiling and how valuable it is to game texturing.

TILING

Why tile? Using a tiling texture obviously has its advantages in games. We've touched on this earlier, and I'm sure that by now, you can imagine the benefit with respect to memory.

In order to understand tiling, remember that texture space is the zone that a texture fits in. The 0-to-1 coordinates bound the range of texture space. Any texture's coordinates extending beyond this range will result in a tiling or repeating texture. Any texture's coordinates that fall short of this range will be stretched and zoomed.

Let's look at a large grassy area as an example (see Figure 5.34). I've dropped in a few placeholder buildings for scale reference.

Without tiling, you would have to create one gigantic texture that covers the entire field in order to maintain your pixel resolution in the scene. In this example, we'd be talking something like 2048×2048 for it to look good. Obviously, this is not the most game-friendly texture. The alternative, and preferred, method is to create a small texture that's tilable and repeat it over the field, keeping your pixel resolution tight and saving tons of texture memory. Figure 5.35 shows a 256×256 texture tiled across the field five times in U and five times in V.

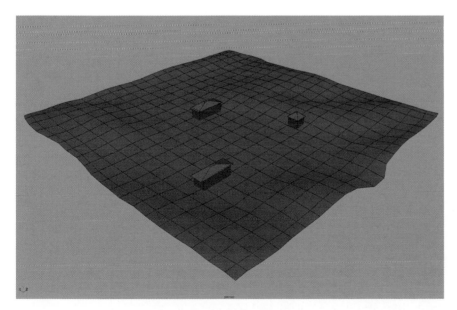

5.34 A grassy field that needs a texture.

5.35 A 256×256 texture is tiled five times in each direction across the mesh.

It works well here, but if you don't know how to create a texture that tiles well, it can look very bad. The most obvious potential problem is visual repetition. If your grass texture is not designed to tile well, you'll see very apparent edges and repeating patterns across the entire area. I'm sure most of you have seen this phenomenon in past games. It can actually look pretty bad if not addressed. If you want a texture to tile well, it has to be somewhat generic. Having distinct markings or obvious shapes will accentuate the repetition and make it apparent that you are tiling. Take a look at the example shown in Figure 5.36, where I added a dark center to the grass texture.

5.36 With the distinct dark center, it becomes obvious that the grass texture is tiling.

So, although it's important to make sure that you texture tiles well by eliminating prominent features or markings, you want to keep the texture as interesting as possible. There are also several tricks you can do to minimize the repeating patterns, which we'll discuss in the tricks and tips chapter (see Chapter 10, "Tips and Tricks").

We have now seen how a seamless, tilable texture is a much more efficient choice than one large texture that covers a huge area. As you are texturing, think carefully about where you can use tiling. Brick walls, floor tiles, grass, and dirt are all good examples of textures that are easily tiled. It all comes back to efficiency; the more tiling you can get away with, the more texture memory you'll have left for the areas that require more detail.

HOW DO YOU TILE?

There are two ways to tile in most 3D packages. First, you can tile the UVs within the material itself. Materials and shaders offer the chance to globally change the tiling of your material. This means that because the tiling information is input at the material level, everywhere that texture appears will be tiled. But what if you don't want that? Well, that is when you tile the individual UV coordinates on a per-object basis to decide when and how much to tile for each object. This is a much more flexible approach because it gives you control over each object. To further clarify, you can either tile the material globally, or you can tile each individual object's UV coordinates to get more precise control.

In most 3D programs, you'll have both options for tiling. The option for tiling globally will be in the material itself, whereas the per-object tiling can be done manually with a UV manipulator or by typing in specific numbers for that manipulator. The per-object tiling option comes up automatically when you assign any type of projection map (see Figure 5.37).

The power of UV mapping is in its flexibility and straightforward logic. Although it has its limits, new tools and features are constantly being added to improve its control and ease of use. A great example of this is the capability to assign multiple sets of UV coordinates to one model.

5.37 The UV manipulator in Maya. You'll find a similar manipulator in 3ds max called the Gizmo.

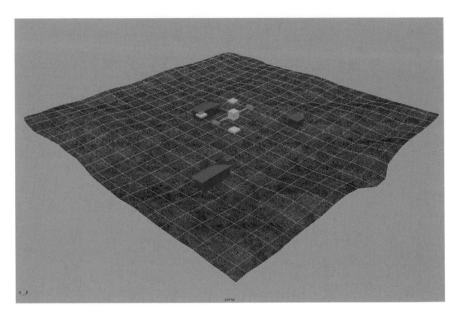

CONCLUSION

So now you know how to paint and create exceptional textures, build efficient polygonal models to assign them to, and control UVs to perfect the final product. It's important to realize that virtually anything you can imagine can be done—it just takes some creative thinking and logical planning. The next chapter is going to bring all these elements together and enable you to create scenes that combine modeling and texturing in a way that takes full advantage of all the lessons learned so far. Let's talk about some advanced modeling techniques.

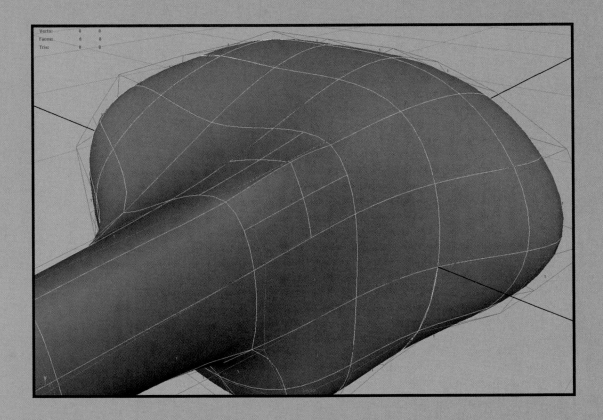

Verts: 0   0
Faces: 0   0
Tris: 0   0

6

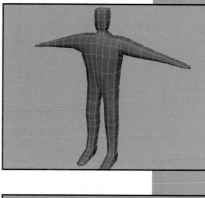

ADVANCED MODELING

THE FOCUS OF THIS CHAPTER will be to go into more depth on game modeling practices and methods. Like most anything else, becoming a skilled game modeler takes not only time and practice, but also the ability to constantly problem solve. As I'm sure you are already aware, being a 3D artist of any kind requires the simultaneous presence of problem-solving skills and artistic talent; sort of a left brain/right brain scenario, which not everyone can easily balance. I think that balance is what I find so intriguing and exciting about creating worlds and objects in 3D. Work, no matter what type, is rarely fun without challenges. And modeling for 3D games presents us with plenty of situations that will keep us on our toes.

In Chapter 2, "Modeling Theory," we discussed the basic idea of polygonal modeling and pointed out some common mistakes to avoid. Now I want to take a closer look at some of the specific techniques that are regularly used in the industry, and offer you some shortcuts that will help you stand out as a game modeler. Making simple primitive shapes and tweaking vertices is one thing. But what do you do when you are faced with the challenge of modeling complex, organic shapes or large-scale terrains? In this chapter, we'll discuss different modeling methods that will give you the tools you need to model almost anything.

ORGANIC VERSUS INORGANIC MODELS

It should be obvious that with polygons, it's easier to create boxy, rigid, inorganic shapes than it is to create smooth, soft shapes. It should also be apparent, then, that you'll have to spend a few more polys to get a shape to look more natural. With games continually becoming more complex and detailed, and with next generation hardware quickly on its way, the expectation for more realistic and organic geometry is increasing. As a modeler, you'll always be exposed to different types of objects ranging from simple and boxy to smooth and complex. But as the computing power increases, you'll need the right tools and techniques to build organically. Let's take a look at some of the methods you can use to create more smooth and naturally organic models.

ORGANIC MODELING METHODS

We covered several methods of simple and rigid box modeling in Chapter 2, so let's take a look at some different ways to build models that are more smooth and organic.

SMOOTHING

One of the most common modeling techniques for creating organic geometry is smoothing. Basically, the process starts with simple box models, blocking out the basic shape. Then, a polygon smooth operation takes that basic shape and smoothes it out by subdividing the geometry. It's a great way to work with broad strokes, taking your time adding detail until you have the desired result.

SMOOTH

Let's start with an example of this method used to build a generic character body in Maya. Figure 6.1 shows a simple cube as the starting point.

Starting with a polygonal cube, and using a simple box modeling technique, we want to extrude faces outward and block out the basic shape of a body (see Figure 6.2). It doesn't have to be too complex; just the major features need to be present.

With the basic shape defined, choose Polygons>Smooth (in the Options window). Let's look at the options. Figure 6.3 displays the options for smoothing.

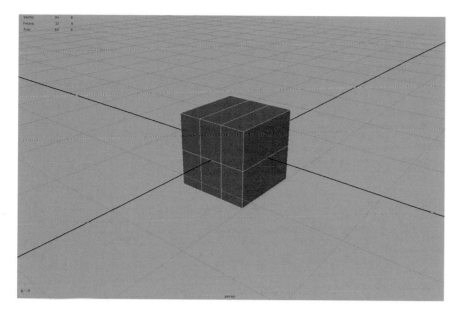

6.1 Start with a basic cube.

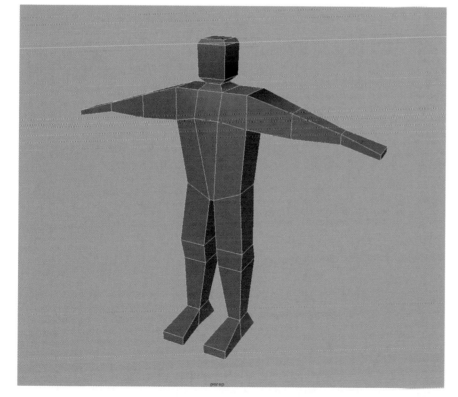

6.2 Extrude the basic shape of a body.

6.3 Smooth Options.

I typically choose Exponential as the subdivision method. The Exponential and Linear smoothing methods both smooth equally, but they offer different controls for the resulting geometry. Exponential has an option to maintain soft and hard edges, whereas Linear has options to better control the number of resulting faces. I always start with a subdivision level of 1. Figure 6.4 shows the result.

Smoothing takes the basic boxy shape and converts it into a more complex and smooth piece of geometry. More importantly, it maintains a solid and consistently grid-like mesh that serves as a great generic starting point for a character model. The more time you spend adding the detail at the boxy stage, the more finished your model will appear when you smooth it. And each time you smooth the model, you can refine the verts until you have an accurate representation.

MESHSMOOTH

In 3ds max you can smooth your geometry by using the MeshSmooth Modifier. It offers control over how your geometry is subdivided, similar to that which we saw with Maya. Again, I always start with one iteration and work my way up from there (see Figure 6.5).

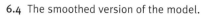

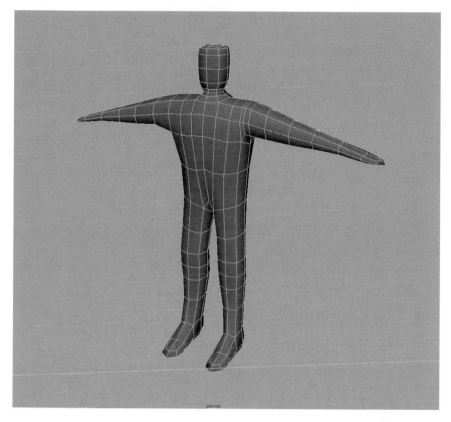

6.4 The smoothed version of the model.

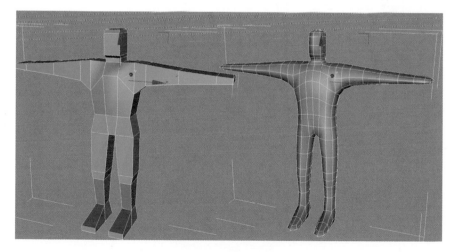

6.5 MeshSmooth in 3ds max subdivides and smoothes your model.

Although the smoothing method is very effective and produces great results, you always run the risk of adding more polys than you really need. Also remember that the fewer polys your box model utilizes, the fewer your smoothed model will have, so start as simple as possible and keep your eye on the poly count as you work. I highly suggest spending some time experimenting with smoothing. You'll find it very handy for all kinds of situations.

THE SCULPT POLYGONS TOOL

Another powerful tool for generating organic geometry quickly and easily is the Sculpt Polygons tool in Maya. Designed with the artist in mind, this tool offers a natural approach to modeling that is more similar to sculpting with clay than rigid 3D geometry. The Sculpt Polygons tool is an artisan-style set of brushes you can use to push, pull, and smooth geometry as opposed to pulling individual verts and faces. This comes in particularly handy for modeling large pieces of organic terrain. It helps to use a Wacom tablet with this tool. You'll find it's much more effective and intuitive than a mouse.

Let's look at an example. We'll start with a simple plane, subdivisions, 30×30 (see Figure 6.6).

Flat terrain is boring, so we need to give it some character. Go to Edit Polygons>Sculpt Polygons Tool (options). Figure 6.7 shows the options.

6.6 A polygonal plane with 30 subdivisions in each direction will serve as our terrain.

This tool has many options. I'll point out a few of the most important features in the following list, but I encourage you to mess around with them later and experiment.

- Stamp Profile—First you choose your brush size. The Brush size is actually called the Stamp Profile.

  - Radius—In order to change the size, adjust the Inner and Outer Radius sliders at the top of the window.

  - Opacity—Opacity functions just like the opacity of a brush in Photoshop; it gives you control over how effective the brush will be on the surface. I usually leave this setting at 1.0 and make adjustments to the Strength option, which I'll discuss in a minute.

- Shape—There are several brush shapes you can choose from.

- Operation—Operation sets how you want the brush to sculpt the surface. I've chosen Pull, so I can pull up some hills around the edge of the terrain.

- Auto Smooth—Auto Smooth is exactly what it sounds like: While you are sculpting, the Auto Smooth setting keeps the effect on the geometry subtle and more organic. I typically keep Auto Smooth on. The Strength setting determines how smooth your strokes will be. Use this to increase or decrease the effect of the smoothing on the geometry.

- Sculpt Variables—Below Strength, you have Sculpt Variables. I leave the Ref. Vector as Normal. What really makes a difference here is the Max Displacement setting. This determines the maximum amount the brush can deform the terrain.

6.7 The Sculpt Polygons Tool options.

Let's take a look at what these settings can do for us.

1. In Figure 6.8, I paint along the edges of the plane, which causes the mesh to be pulled (deformed, displaced) up in the Y direction.

2. Now I'll use the Push operation to lay in some valleys (see Figure 6.9).

3. Now I'll use the Smooth operation to further refine the peaks and valleys. Smooth subtly softens the drastic changes in the geometry by scaling the Y values closer together (see Figure 6.10).

6.8 Using the Pull operation to deform the terrain by painting.

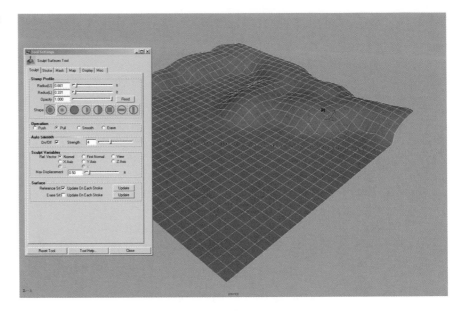

6.9 The Push operation.

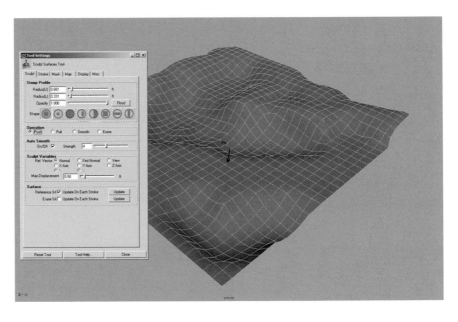

By using only these three operations, you can quickly pull up hillsides, indent a lake or stream, or smooth your overall terrain.

The Erase feature is also great because it will flatten out an area that you may have previously sculpted, down to its original position. It works great for carving out a road through some hills (see Figure 6.11).

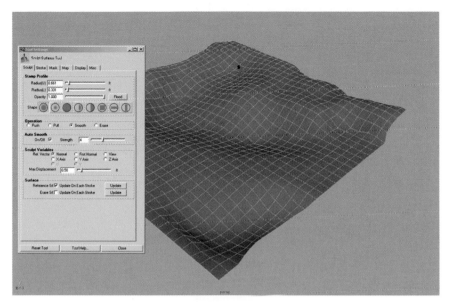

6.10 Using the Smooth operation to soften the peaks and valleys.

6.11 Erase essentially undoes your deformations and flattens the geometry back out to its original position.

SOFT SELECTION

Although 3ds max does not have a Sculpt Polygons tool, it does have a powerful feature that Maya lacks, which does a fantastic job of modeling organic terrain out of polygons. It's called Soft Selection, and it can be found in the Modify panel when you are in Vertex Editing mode. Let's look at a simple plane again. Figure 6.12 shows the plane.

6.12 A polygonal plane.

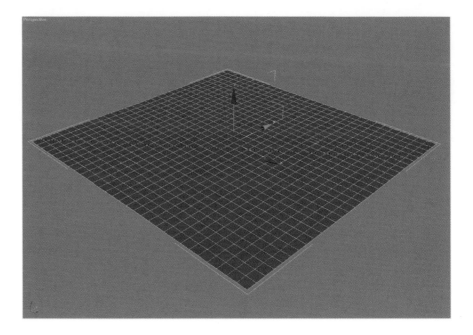

Go to Sub-object mode and choose Verts. Now expand the Soft Selection rollout. Check the Use Soft Selection box (see Figure 6.13).

Grab some verts on the mesh, and you'll notice multicolored verts acting as highlights around your selection. The surrounding verts will be transformed along with your selection, but to a lesser degree based on distance or "falloff." Change the Falloff value and you'll see the selection change accordingly. You can see this in Figure 6.14.

Now when we move the verts upward, you'll see the model result is much more organic and natural (see Figure 6.15).

Soft Selection is a valuable feature that can save you a tremendous amount of time by giving you more subtle control while editing verts.

The Use Soft Selection check box.

6.13 Soft Selection.

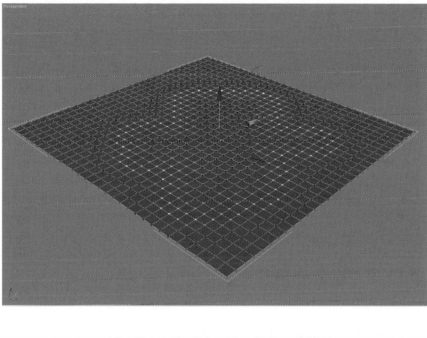

6.14 Vertex falloff.

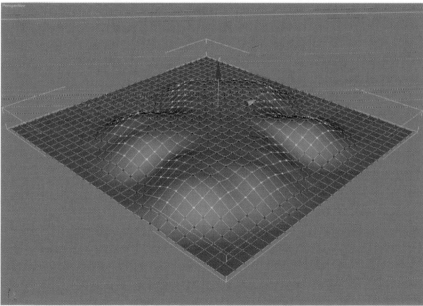

6.15 Using Soft Selection in max to deform geometry more organically.

SUBDIVISION SURFACES

As we have discussed to this point, polygons are the current geometry type used for modeling in games. Although polygons are a powerful and efficient toolset, there are of course advantages to other types of geometry. And you can be sure that polygons will not always be the most common type. With the next generation of hardware approaching quickly, and the quality standards of games increasing exponentially, you can count on subdivision (SubD or Subdiv) surfaces to play a large role in game modeling and possibly be the preferred geometry type for many of the new games you will see in the coming years. Even now, SubD surfaces are used frequently to build complex geometry, and then are easily converted to polygons to use in games. Similar in some ways to the smoothing approach, SubD surface modeling takes that concept to new heights. It offers ways of creating details that can be very difficult and time-consuming (if not impossible) with polygons. You can count on SubD and other geometry types to be used in future games, so it's important to learn the tools now so you can easily transition into the next generation as an artist.

The power of SubD surface modeling is in its unique characteristics. You can think of SubD as a hybrid of different geometry types. It takes many of the advantages of NURBS and polygonal modeling and wraps them into one powerful and useful set of tools. You can edit SubD with the same methods available to you with polygonal tools (extrude, translating verts, and so on), as well as the specific SubD tools like crease and detail levels. Let's take a look at how SubD surfaces work.

I'll start by creating a Subdivision Surfaces Cube in Maya by choosing Create>Subdiv Primitives>Cube (see Figure 6.16).

> **TIP**
>
> Keep in mind, you can also create polygonal geometry and convert it to SubD with the same result.

You'll probably notice that the cube doesn't look exactly like the type of cube we are accustomed to. This is because of smooth display levels. SubD essentially smoothes your geometry, but maintains the original primitive shape. You just have to toggle smooth displays to see the difference. This can be done by hitting the 2 and 3 keys in Maya. The 3 key will provide a more smooth representation of the mesh in the viewport (see Figure 6.17).

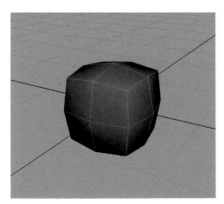

6.16 A SubD cube.

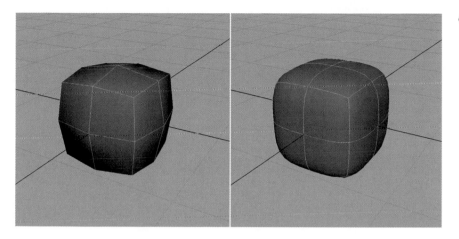

6.17 Different smooth values on the same cube.

So now we have a subdivision surface; what can we do with it? Well, you can edit the components of a SubD surface just like polygons. Grab a vertex or face and translate away (see Figure 6.18).

You'll instantly see the difference between polys and SubDs; the SubD surface acts more like a NURBS object, with smooth interpolated curves as opposed to the harsh angles you get when pulling verts on polygons. This obviously gives the modeler an advantage when creating organic shapes.

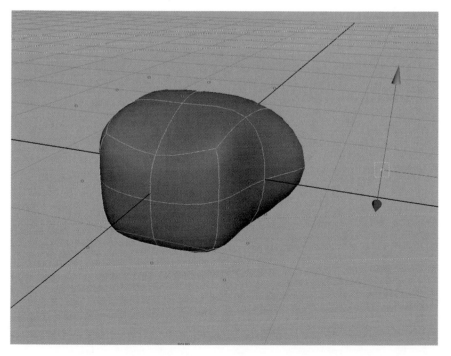

6.18 Editing the SubD surface.

But let's say that we realize we should have made some major adjustments when we first started with the cube shape. Here is where another advantage of SubD comes in. SubD surfaces have two editing modes, Standard and Polygon. So far we have only looked at the Standard mode, which is the default mode for editing SubD geometry. But if we switch to Polygon editing mode (by right-clicking on the object and choosing Polygon), you'll see we now have control of a polygonal cage made up of verts, faces, and edges that deforms the SubD surface. In Figure 6.19 you see I've gone into Polygon editing mode and extruded a face at the polygon level.

So, what we are basically able to do is edit a complex and smooth piece of geometry with a simple and manageable polygonal cage.

To point out another advantage to SubD, I'm going to select an edge in Polygonal editing mode. Now I'll choose Subdiv Surfaces>Full Crease Edge/Vertex (see Figure 6.20)

Because SubD geometry is inherently organic, the Crease and Uncrease tool lets you choose which edges are sharp and angular and which are smooth.

The advantage is clear: being able to work on your model with broad strokes or fine detail while having the opportunity to switch back and forth any time. It's like an oil painting that allows you to go back and change the colors underneath the surface layer of paint whenever you feel like it.

TIP

You can also change the complexity of the polygonal cage by choosing Coarser or Finer from the right-click menu.

6.19 An extruded face at the Polygon editing level.

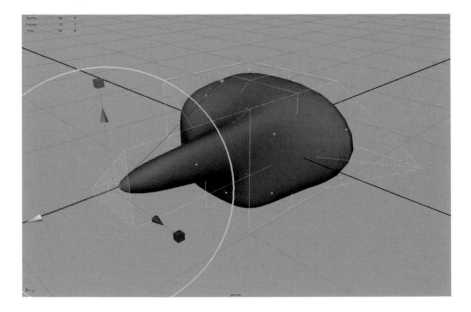

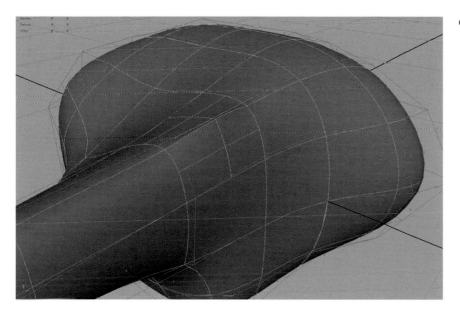

6.20 By using the Crease and Uncrease Edge/Vert option in the Subdiv Surfaces menu, you can define how smooth or rigid your geometry is.

To work with subdivision surfaces in 3ds max, you create polygonal geometry and add an HSDS (Hierarchical Subdivision Surfaces) modifier. The functionality is essentially the same as the example for Maya (see Figure 6.21).

You can see the power of subdivision surfaces and how they can expedite the modeling process. Just because SubD is not currently used in game geometry, don't forget that you can always model in SubD, and then convert to polygons in the end.

CONVERTING SUBDIVISION SURFACES TO POLYGONS

The process for converting between geometry types is not typically a complex one, although some types of geometry tend to convert more predictably and reliably than others. SubD to polygons is a great example of this. To convert from SubD to polys in Maya, go to Modify> Convert>Subdiv to Polygons. The options box has several choices (see Figure 6.22).

There are four tessellation methods to choose from. I always use Adaptive, which does its best to keep the geometry as similar as possible in shape and size. You also have the option to tessellate by Polygon Count or number of Vertices, if you know your model has to be a certain resolution. Figure 6.23 shows the poly version of the SubD model.

6.21 The HSDS modifier in 3ds max converts a polygonal object into a subdivision surface.

6.22 The Convert Subdiv to Polygons Options in Maya.

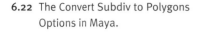

6.22 The Convert Subdiv to Polygons Options in Maya.

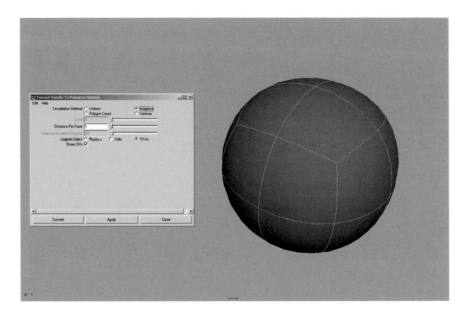

VERTEX NORMALS AND SMOOTHING GROUPS

Another key to ensuring your geometry looks as smooth and detailed as possible is by adjusting the vertex normals to change the way your object appears and reacts to light. (This is also discussed more in Chapter 8, "In-Game Lighting.")

Vertex normals are similar to face normals in that they provide the renderer with information about that vertex's position and orientation. When edges meet at a vertex, they can either have a shared vertex normal or a split vertex normal. Let's take a look at the difference. Figure 6.24 shows a sphere with its split (or unshared) vertex normals displayed. There are four edges meeting at each vertex, so there are four separate vertex normals at each junction. You can see in Figure 6.24 that the effect on the sphere is to make it faceted and boxy.

6.23 The converted polygon sphere.

Maybe this is what you want if you are modeling a disco ball, but if we want the sphere to appear smooth, we need to share the vertices. Keep in mind, this does not change the geometry in any way; we are simply adjusting the vertex normals to change the way the surface appears. However, it's important to remember that if you split the vertex normals into four, you are essentially increasing the size of the mesh by 4× in the engine. In Maya, there is a feature called Soften/Harden (Edit Polygons> Normals>Soften/Harden) that allows you to set the vertex normals based on a threshold (see Figure 6.25).

The threshold ranges from 0 (split normals) to 180 (shared normals). Take a look at the difference in Figure 6.26, where I set the vertices to be shared and smooth.

6.24 A sphere with its vertex normals displayed and not smoothed.

6.25 The Soften/Harden feature in Maya allows you to manipulate your vertex normals to define a smooth or faceted appearance.

6.26 Shared vertex normals give the geometry a smooth appearance.

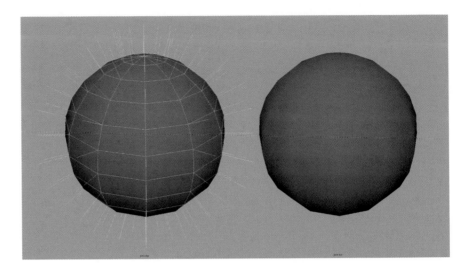

Vertex normals are an important part of polygonal modeling because, along with texture, they help establish the surface characteristics of your geometry. Oftentimes you'll find it is to your advantage to have a mixture of soft and hard areas in your model to help define the detail of the surfaces.

Each software package deals with vertex normals differently, but it's rare that you'll need to actually manipulate each individual vertex normal. 3ds max uses what are called smoothing groups. Smoothing eliminates the facets on geometry by grouping faces into groups. Faces in the same smoothing group appear as a smooth surface.

To tweak vertex normals in 3ds max, use a modifier called Smooth (not to be confused with MeshSmooth, discussed earlier). The Smooth modifier uses the same threshold as the one used in Maya's Soften/Harden, from 0 to 180. Keep in mind that in order to adjust the threshold, you need to check the Auto Smooth box. Figure 6.27 shows an example of the use of the Smooth modifier.

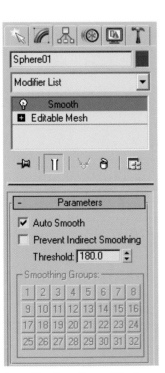

6.27 The Smooth modifier in max lets you set the angle of the vertex normals.

MODELING WITH TRIANGLES

Remember that all polygonal geometry is made up of triangles, and the reason we see quads is because the triangles are hidden by default in order to make working with the model easier and less jumbled. As I mentioned briefly in Chapter 2, sometimes it is advantageous to model with your triangle edges visible as opposed to the default quad façade. Edge placement is often crucial in determining the shape of a polygonal object.

As your models become more complex and your poly counts increase, you'll find it more and more difficult to keep your mesh clean and stable. In certain cases, looking closely at the internal structure of triangles in your model will help you ensure that it is as clean as can be.

Another advantage to working with triangle edges is that you have the option to turn or flip tri edges. There are several reasons why this is beneficial. As an example, the placement or orientation of an edge on a polygonal face could determine the placement of the bridge of a nose or the placement of the cheeks. Take a look at the default sphere shown in Figure 6.28 with triangle edges visible; you can see that they are all facing the same direction. By flipping certain tri edges, you can actually manipulate the geometry in ways that were not possible with the previous version of the sphere.

As you can see, using your triangle edges gives you more flexibility and control over the model. To access the triangle edges in Maya, go to Polygons>Triangulate. It will display the tris and allow you to select them as edges. To Flip an edge, select it and go to Edit Polygons>Flip Triangle Edge.

To do the same in 3ds max, with the object selected, go to the Display panel and uncheck the Edges Only box. Figure 6.29 shows the Edges Only check box. Now go to the Modify panel, and while in Edge Mode, press the Turn button (see Figure 6.30). Now you are in Turn Edges mode. Every edge that you click on will flip.

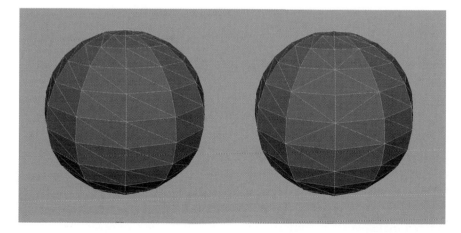

6.28 By flipping or turning triangle edges, you have more control over the resulting geometry.

TIP

The extra control you get over your model by using the triangle edges can also be harnessed by using tools like the Split Polygon tool in Maya (Edit Polygons>Split Polygon Tool) or the Cut Faces tool in max (in Face or Edge mode, choose Cut). The idea is simple: You click and drag lines across faces to establish new edges. This can be very useful for cutting out shapes, or just for adding detail to a model where necessary.

The Edges Only check box

The Turn button

6.29 In the Display panel, uncheck the Edges Only box to make the triangle edges visible.

6.30 The Turn button puts you into Turn Edges mode.

The important thing to remember when using these tools is to be very careful not to create abnormal faces, T-junctions, or floating verts. Always be sure that when you lay down new points, they are snapping to the existing vertices, and you'll be safe.

CLEANING UP YOUR GEOMETRY

When your model is complete, it's time to export your work into a game engine. The process and tools differ from project to project, but the idea is simple. You model, texture, and light within your 3D software and then export that scene or individual model into the game engine. If you are lucky, you'll have a development machine on your desk that allows you to view your model in the game instantly. But before you export, it's always a good idea to check and double-check the model to make sure that it is not only efficient, but also clean, and will not cause errors. I've mentioned this before, but what you see in Maya or 3ds max is not always what you will see in the game engine. Many times you'll see reversed normals, distorted geometry, or even nothing at all. We talked about common mistakes in Chapter 2, and there could be a thousand other reasons for these problems, but your job as an artist is to adhere to the guidelines given to you by the programmers and to ensure that the models you create are as clean as possible. Many art pipelines have safeguards built into them that will give the artist an error message when exporting to the engine if anything is not to spec. Maybe there are floating verts, or a texture is the wrong size. I'd like to point out a few practices you can adopt to help make sure that the models you are creating can hold up as solid, game-ready art.

DELETE HISTORY

Get in the habit of frequently deleting the history on your objects (in 3ds max this is called Collapsing the Stack or Converting to Editable Mesh). History is basically the list of things you have done to the model as you continue to work. The list grows very quickly, and the more history on your object, the more unstable it will be. It's difficult for 3D software to keep track of all that information, and it often causes the geometry to become messy and inefficient. Not to mention that history and game engines do not get along well at all. So start to train yourself now; put a sticky note on your monitor as a reminder. Always delete history!

In Maya, go to Edit>Delete by Type>History. In 3ds max, right-click on the object and choose Convert To>Convert To Editable Mesh (see Figure 6.31).

6.31 Deleting history in 3ds max by converting to Editable Mesh.

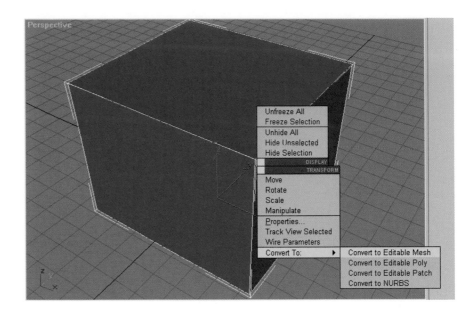

Even though this is a quick and easy way to delete history, it does force you to choose polygonal geometry as your output mesh type. The safe way to delete history without forcing a geometry type is to collapse the stack. To do this, in the Modify panel, right-click on the topmost modifier and choose Collapse All.

FREEZE TRANSFORMATIONS

As you work on your model, translating objects and components, the 3D software sometimes gets confused about where that object is in local and world space. Freezing transformations essentially resets the coordinates of your model and is somewhat of a fresh start.

In Maya, go to Modify>Freeze Transformations. In 3ds max, go to the Hierarchy tab, and under Adjust Transform, click on the Reset Transform button (see Figure 6.32).

CENTER PIVOT

Similar to resetting transformations, as you move objects and components, or add and delete geometry, the center point or pivot of the model becomes skewed. Center Pivot looks at the entire model and chooses a new center. This is important for many game engines that rely on the pivot to place the object in space. In my experience, when I export a model and it is far from where I expected it be, or it doesn't show up at all, my first thought is to make sure that the pivot was centered.

In Maya, go to Modify>Center Pivot. In 3ds max, go to the Hierarchy tab, and under Move/Rotate/Scale, click on the Affect Pivot Only button. Then, under Alignment, click on the Center to Object button (see Figure 6.33).

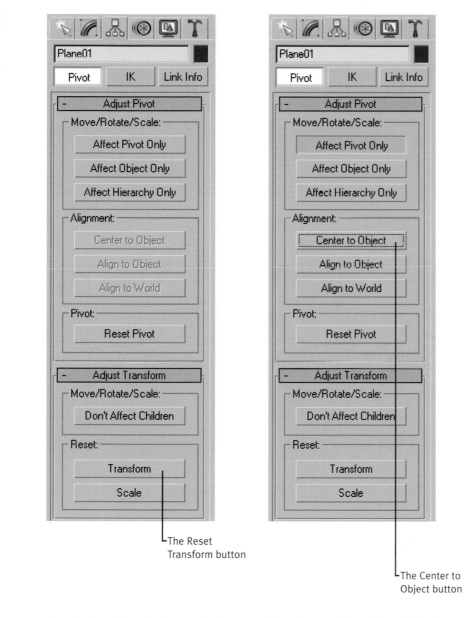

The Reset Transform button

The Center to Object button

6.32 The Reset Transform button in 3ds max.   **6.33** Centering the pivot point in 3ds max.

6.34 Welding verts in 3ds max.

MERGING OR WELDING VERTICES

As you model you'll find that you will be welding individual vertices quite often. But when you feel a model is finished, it's always a good idea to select the entire object and, with a low threshold, merge vertices. Be careful not to set the threshold too high or your geometry will collapse. But by merging the overall model one last time, you'll catch floating and doubled verts that may have eluded you during the modeling process.

To merge vertices in Maya, go to Edit Polygons>Merge Vertices.

> **TIP**
>
> Another trick in Maya is to select all the vertices of the model, then hit the Delete key on your keyboard. This will delete any verts that do not share an edge. Keep in mind that hitting the Delete key is different from choosing Edit Polygons> Delete Vertex. If you select all the verts on a model and use Delete Vertex from the menu, all your verts will be deleted.

In 3ds max, go into Vertex Sub-object mode and select all the mesh's vertices. Under the Edit Geometry panel, you will find a Weld section, which holds a button named Selected with numbers next to it. The numbers indicate a vertex range within which the Weld Selected operation will operate, welding vertices. Set the range you want, and hit the Selected button to weld the vertices (see Figure 6.34).

MAYA'S CLEANUP TOOL

Maya also has a great feature called Polygon Cleanup, which removes different types of problem geometry like four or more sided faces, faces with holes, and concave faces. There are also options to merge vertices, remove unnecessary edges, and conform normals. It's a great tool, and I suggest using it frequently.

CONCLUSION

The line between hi-res renders and games is obviously blurring, and it's going to happen much quicker than most realize. The only thing that is currently separating the two workflows is sheer computing power. And as we have all learned, technology advances exponentially, especially in an industry where the stakes are high and the competition is fierce. Game development is spearheading the drive to make movies and games indistinguishable. So imagine that eight years from now you are modeling with NURBS for a game that is indistinguishable from a prerendered film. The skills and habits you establish today, modeling efficiently and cleanly, are going to make you that much stronger of a modeler in the future.

Now that we've covered everything from reference to advanced modeling, there is only one major element missing: lighting. The next two chapters will focus on lighting and game-specific methods and implementation. Just like all other aspects of 3D, it's important to remember that everything works together, and you should always be thinking about how the big picture will look. Lighting is the icing on the cake!

7

LIGHTING PRINCIPLES

BEFORE WE GET INTO LIGHTING for games specifically, I think it's important to talk about the art of traditional lighting. It won't do us any good to know the tools and procedures if we don't have a strong artistic foundation. There have been hundreds of books written with respect to lighting theory and methodology, so I'll do my best to just touch on the most important aspects in this chapter. But I encourage you to research and learn as much about lighting as you possibly can.

Remember that everything we see around us is light. When you see an apple, you aren't seeing an apple, you are seeing the light that is reflected and bounced off the surface of that apple. Without light, the visual world as we know it does not exist. So, when you as an artist are put in the position of playing God, "Let there be light!," you'd better know what you are doing! Lighting plays a pivotal role in creating atmosphere and mood in a scene. Think about stage lighting for a play, or a dramatic film noir style movie. Lighting alone can conjure feelings and emotions, tell a story, or even drastically change the meaning of what you are seeing.

ABOVE IMAGES © 2003 LUCASFILM ENTERTAINMENT COMPANY LTD. OR LUCASFILM LTD. & ® OR ™ AS INDICATED. ALL RIGHTS RESERVED.

Unless you give your characters and environments appropriate lighting, you can easily blow out and flatten the entire scene, essentially hiding all the beautiful work you have done so far. Whether you are lighting for stage, photography, film, or 3D, the primary function of lighting is to give form to the objects in the scene. The form of a three-dimensional object can be either revealed or hidden depending on how the light hits the object and at what angle with respect to the camera. Keep in mind that defining and highlighting form is the first thing you should think about when lighting. In addition to the primary purpose of defining shape, light can be a story-telling medium, affecting mood, form, color, intensity, and movement. Let's start by talking about color.

Color

Color plays a powerful role in defining mood in a scene. We as artists all know about warm colors and cool colors, complimentary colors, and so on. But the important thing to think about is how color affects the viewer. We tend to instantly fall into the trap of cliché: Red means hot and dangerous; blue means cool and safe. There is no doubt that these colors can evoke those particular emotions and feelings if presented properly, but it is important to remember that you as an artist can evoke any emotion you want with any color. It's about defining rules within your scene and making distinct associations. Look at the movie *The Matrix* as an example. Using two simple hues, blue and green, we the audience were subtly taught whether a scene was taking place in the Matrix or in the real world. Adding that color information, whether you noticed it or not, really helped hold the story together and defined a rule that we were more than happy to follow.

Target Audience

Another aspect of color that you should think about when lighting your scene is your target audience. To most Americans, the color red typically conveys emotions of danger and immediacy. But in China, red conveys happy celebration and evokes entirely different emotions.

To us, white is associated with purity and joy, wedding dresses and baby clothes. In China, white means death. Funeral attire in China is typically white.

Knowing your audience is important to all aspects of artwork, but choosing the right colors with which to light your scene increases your chances of conveying the feeling you want. So you can see that culture and audience play a significant part in choosing color and evoking specific emotions. Figure 7.1 shows an example of the use of red that would work with an American audience.

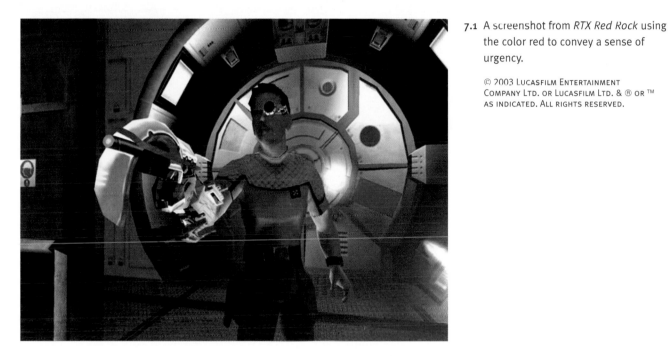

7.1 A screenshot from *RTX Red Rock* using the color red to convey a sense of urgency.

BALANCING COLOR

Choosing the right colors in a scene has to be a balancing act. For those of you who have taken color theory and design classes, you know how dramatic an effect colors can have on one another when seen together. Too many powerful colors and the visual impact becomes chaotic and over-stimulating. Too little, and the work is drab and boring. When lighting, look at your scene as an individual piece of artwork. Be sure your colors are balanced and chosen carefully. Use colors that work well together and don't conflict (unless you want to convey a conflicting situation or emotion). Try to choose and commit to a specific set of colors (color scheme) in your scene that represents the mood you want your audience to feel. Pay close attention to the color scheme of your textures and choose light color accordingly. Figure 7.2 shows a subtle yet effective choice of colors. Notice how color is shared among objects and balanced in the room.

7.2 A subtle and pleasing balance of color in *Star Wars: Knights of the Old Republic.*

MOOD

Along with color, many aspects of lighting help establish mood. Intensity, direction and angle, number of lights, and shadows all play a major role in defining the mood of the scene. Thinking ahead and collecting references will help you capture the feel that you want for your particular scene. Here are a few screenshots from *Star Wars: Knights of the Old Republic* showing different styles used to create a sense of mood and atmosphere. Figure 7.3 shows a soothing outdoor scene that conveys a sense of calm. Figure 7.4 demonstrates how long shadows set the mood.

Lighting effects like rays and beams help further define the atmosphere, suggesting humidity, dust, and air quality. Figure 7.5 shows a successful use of light beams in *Gladius.*

7.3 A calming outdoor scene using simple, yet effective, lighting.

7.4 Long shadows not only add to the atmosphere, but also help break up repetition.

7.5 Light beams and rays give clues as to the humidity, dust, and air quality in a scene.

TRADITIONAL LIGHTING SETUP

Traditional stage lighting and 3D lighting share many similarities, most noticeably types and general placement. It's good to study traditional lighting to form an understanding of how important and effective light can be on your subjects, but be careful not to make the mistake of thinking that 3D lighting is just like real-world lighting. In fact, despite the many successful efforts to simulate real-world lighting in a 3D environment, the way to get there is not always as straightforward as one might think. Light in the real world behaves quite differently than light in a 3D scene. The trick is to use the tools you have to try and create a scene that is as accurate and appealing as possible. The following list lays out a common traditional lighting setup, and then the following section compares it to a 3D setup.

A great way to start lighting is to begin with a traditional setup, then change and build on top of that until you get the desired result. More broad stroke theory!

A successful lighting setup should include at least the following types of lights:

■ Key light—A key light is the main light source in a scene. The key light is usually the most intense light and provides the majority of illumination and direction in the scene. A key light is best positioned at an angle with respect to the objects and camera to define the 3D forms. Figure 7.6 exemplifies a sphere with a key light only. We can see the direction, but the rest of the sphere is completely black and lost in the background.

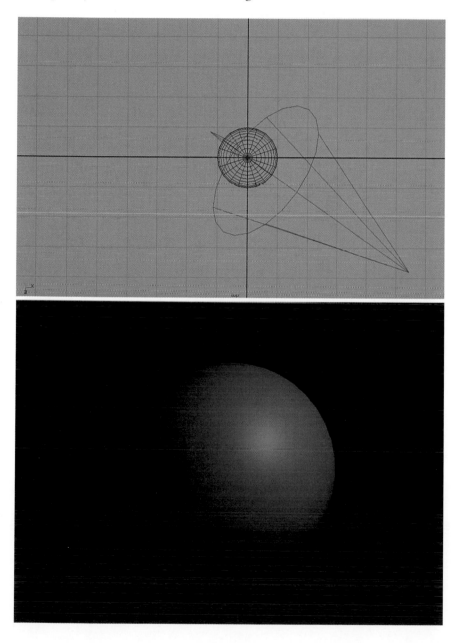

7.6 A sphere lit only by a key light positioned at an angle. The detail and form of the sphere are not as clear as if we added another light source.

■ Fill light—Just like it sounds, a fill light brings out some of the shadow detail while still giving the object its form. A fill light is meant to bring out the details that are lost in shadow. Fill light works well at an angle alternate to that of the key light. You can see how a fill light more clearly defines the form of the sphere in Figure 7.7.

7.7 A fill light brings out more form. Notice the point light has been added to the left of the sphere.

The new point light ————

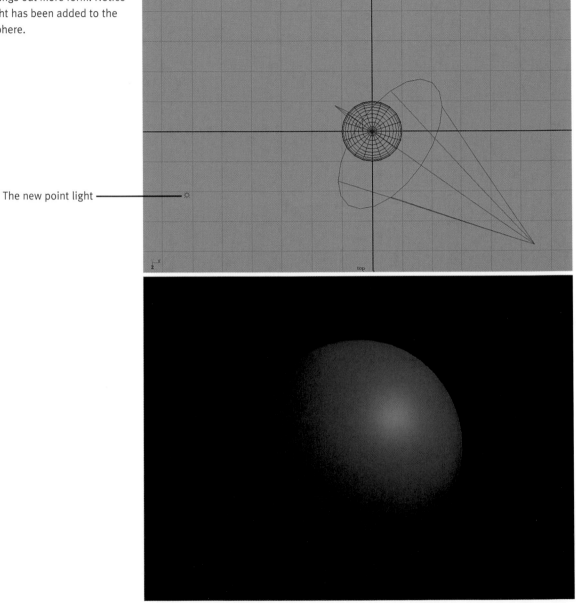

■ Backlight (rim light)—A backlight is placed behind and slightly above or below the object to again help define the shape of the object. The backlight highlights the edges of an object and pulls it away from the background. Figure 7.8 shows the sphere with a backlight.

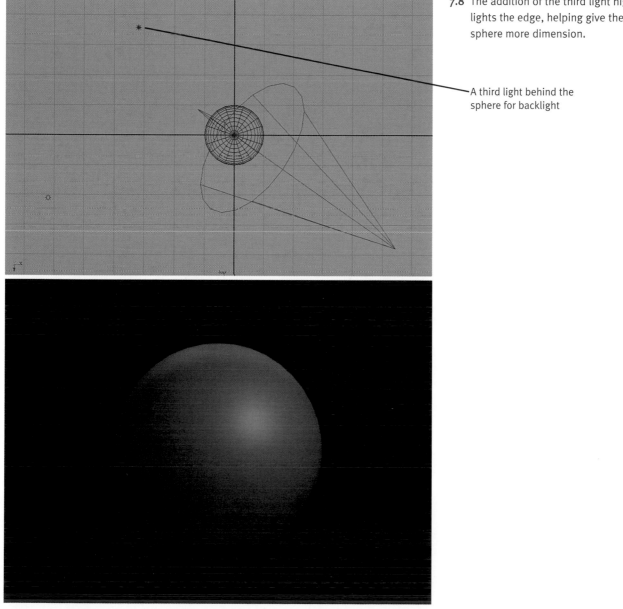

7.8 The addition of the third light highlights the edge, helping give the sphere more dimension.

A third light behind the sphere for backlight

A simple three-light setup like this is a good way to start lighting in 3D. It's easy to get carried away when lighting and start to add tons of lights. This is typically not a good idea, not only because it gets confusing and causes a larger file size, but also because lights tend to add on top of one another until you have a completely blown-out scene. That's why we start with a simple setup and gradually add the details we need. Sound familiar?

WORKING WITH 3D LIGHTS

Most 3D packages offer the same types of light despite different naming and iconic representation. The important thing to remember when lighting in a 3D environment is that the lights you are using are simply an attempt to simulate lighting in the real world. Think about traditional lighting setups as you start to work in 3D. It will give you a solid foundation to work with and you'll be surprised how effective even a three-light setup can be. Next we'll discuss the most commonly used lights in 3D.

DIRECTIONAL LIGHT

Directional lights (see Figure 7.9) are most often used to simulate sunlight and moonlight. Typically functioning as a key light in a scene, they provide controllable and predictable illumination. Due to the fact that the sun is so far away from the earth, by the time the light reaches us, the rays are essentially parallel to one another (see Figure 7.10). That is why you will also hear the term *parallel light* when referring to directional lights. The farther away the light source, the more parallel the rays become. Directional lights do not fall off with distance; the intensity is constant everywhere in the scene.

AMBIENT LIGHT

Ambient light (see Figure 7.11) is light that is spread everywhere equally in all directions without dissipating with distance. Although no true ambient light exists in the real world, its general purpose in 3D is to simulate the bounced light that occurs all around us. Essentially, it serves as a fill light. Computers are powerful, but to calculate every ray of light as it bounces off every object and changes color, intensity, and direction results in dramatically increased render time. We are using ambient light to simulate the bounced light due to

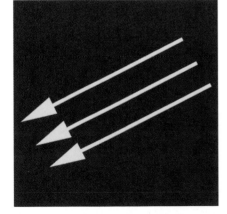

7.9 A typical representation of a 3D directional light.

7.10 By the time the sun's rays reach the earth, they are nearly parallel to one another.

the computational burden of actually raytracing or using radiosity lighting. Use very low intensity ambient light to create a uniform diffuse light in your scene.

SPOTLIGHTS

One of the most commonly used lights in 3D is a spotlight (see Figure 7.12) because of the amount of control the artist has over its parameters and variety of effects. Spotlights are often the key light in a scene as well. Of course, in the most traditional sense, a spotlight is what we think of when we envision a stage with a single performer in a focused conical beam of light, and it works very well for that exact situation. But spotlights can provide lighting solutions for an endless amount of situations.

POINT OR OMNI LIGHTS

Just like it sounds, a point light (see Figure 7.13) emits from a single point in all directions. Also referred to as a uniform light, it is ideal for lightbulbs, lamps, candles, and the like. Point lights are extremely flexible and do a great job of producing these types of lighting effects.

You will find many additional types of lights in various 3D packages. Each is a variation of the core types discussed here. Each is designed to serve specific purposes. You will encounter lights such as area lights, volume lights, skylights, and sunlight systems. Play around with each

7.11 An ambient light.

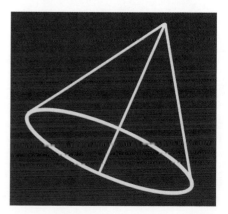

7.12 A spotlight.

7.13 A point light.

of them and you'll quickly discover their individual purposes even though their functionality doesn't stray much from the light types discussed here.

GLOBAL ILLUMINATION

Global illumination attempts to more accurately re-create real-world lighting by calculating the bounced light from all surfaces. In real life, light not only emits from light sources such as lamps, candles, or the sun, but also every object in the environment reflects and emits its own light, adding to the overall illumination of the scene. Raytracing was one of the first global illumination algorithms developed to emulate this type of lighting. Although raytracing can do a nice job of calculating bounced light and accurate shadows, it is extremely slow and lacks the softness and accuracy of other more recent solutions such as radiosity. Radiosity renderers also calculate global illumination by taking indirect light, surface properties, and specularity into account, creating a much more realistic scene. Figure 7.14 shows a room lit without and with a radiosity solution.

In Chapter 4, "Advanced Texturing," we talked about the surface properties of materials, such as specularity and bump mapping. It's important to point out that the surface characteristics have a significant effect on lighting. Lighting can affect objects with varying surface properties in drastically different ways.

Although the term *global illumination* is somewhat generic, just remember that it is essentially an attempt at bouncing and reflecting light in a scene to better simulate real-world behavior. Also keep in mind that as light bounces off objects, it picks up the color of those objects and carries it through the rest of the scene. Using small, low intensity colored lights is a great way to simulate this principle.

FALLOFF

Sometimes called attenuation, falloff limits the distance light will travel from its source. Falloff is commonly localized to affect only the surrounding objects, controlling where the light shines. Falloff can be applied to any type of light we discussed and is very advantageous, especially when it comes to lighting 3D objects. Having the ability to contain and control where your light travels and how it illuminates your scene gives you the precision you need as an artist. 3ds max has a great representation of falloff that shows you exactly where your light will be contained (see Figure 7.15).

7.14 Top: A room lit without radiosity. Bottom: The same room with a radiosity solution.

© 2004 Eric Schuck.
Courtesy of Ilusionations.

When you choose to use falloff on your lights for vertex lighting purposes, you'll find that you'll need to compensate by increasing the intensity to maintain the original brightness. It's not uncommon to have to increase the intensity by 50% or more.

7.15 Falloff (attenuation) visually represented in 3ds max.

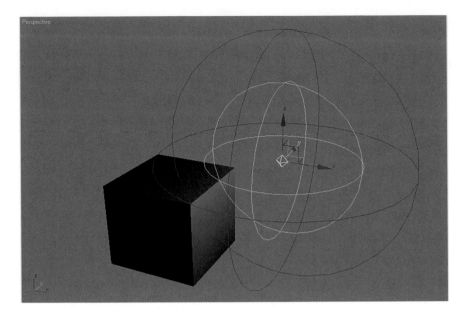

EFFECTIVE LIGHTING PRACTICES

There are a few tricks I've learned in my experience with 3D lighting that I have found very useful and effective.

POOLS OF LIGHT

Lighting your scene using small areas of light (I like to call them pools of light) gives a scene much more depth and character. As opposed to lighting objects uniformly, try to break up the surfaces by using these smaller spheres of light to focus attention on the important elements in the scene. The pools also add a slight sense of mystery and apprehension because you might not know what could be lurking in that dark corner. Figure 7.16 provides an example in which pools of light are used well.

When lighting for games in particular, you'll find that light is extremely important to gameplay. For example, the areas you illuminate and draw attention to can be clues to the player. What door should I go in? Where is the hidden passageway? Questions like this can easily be answered with the proper lighting. Remember that you have the power to set ground rules and guide the player through a game with light (see Figure 7.17). Get in the habit of thinking about how a player moves through your scene. You can have the best-looking lighting in the world, but if it doesn't collaborate with gameplay, the point is lost.

7.16 Pools of light in *Indiana Jones: The Emperor's Tomb*.

7.17 Using light to guide the player helps highlight areas that are accessible and important to the objectives.

Be Creative

If you really want to excel at lighting, try not to stick to the standard solutions. Put some thought into the history and purpose of your scene. Just like texturing, giving some intelligent thought to what you are doing provides the opportunity to tell a story with your lights. It's not just about making it look good; it's about using your artistic license to take a concept to the next level. Take the initiative to talk in depth with the level designer and art director to find out where that scene falls into the grand scheme of things. Maybe the level before yours was meant to be relatively easy and relaxing, but your level is supposed to challenge and intimidate the player, bringing them back into the action. It is your responsibility as an artist to convey that tension and immersion required to make the gameplay effective.

Experiment

I usually start with a simple lighting setup and add detail as I go along. But in the early stages, I like to experiment with different colors and positions for the lights. I can't tell you how many times I've stumbled upon a great lighting scenario by just taking some chances and seeing what it looks like. Try crazy combinations of color, reverse the intensities, or reposition lights in unorthodox places. Just keep in mind the purpose of the scene that you are creating and do your best to accentuate and improvise.

Conclusion

When thinking about lighting, the best thing you can do is closely study real-world lighting situations. Thinking and analyzing how light works around you will help you understand how light works and help you see the potential of the tools you have available to you in a 3D environment. I can't say this enough, but you have to remember that the lights you create in 3D are at best a very simplified and limited representation of real light. In order to simulate real-world lighting, you really have to understand the tools you have to work with and find creative solutions that give you the result you are looking for.

Take a photo and spend the time to analyze the lighting scenario taking place in the scene. Choose an area outside that you can visit and take notes at different times of the day, when it's sunny, overcast, raining, and so on. Focusing on a familiar area will give you the chance to really document and analyze the subtle changes that take place.

As you walk around during the day (or night) look not only at the lighting around you, but also for the light sources, and think about how they are influencing what you are seeing. Look for color, direction, specular highlights, intensity, and so on. This goes back to reference and its ability to provide you with information you would never be able to imagine on your own. Look at film and artwork that catches your eye and analyze what is happening with the lighting. The key to developing your skills as a lighting artist is to rely on your ability to observe and re-create what you see around you using the tools at hand. In the next chapter, we will take these ideas and apply them even more specifically to lighting for games.

Medal of Honor Frontline™ IMAGES COURTESY OF ELECTRONIC ARTS INC. © 2002 ELECTRONIC ARTS INC. ALL RIGHTS RESERVED.

8

IN-GAME LIGHTING

SEVERAL METHODS ARE USED to create lighting in today's games. All of them are quite intriguing and creative solutions. Lighting for games is one of the more challenging aspects of game art because the computing power required to calculate accurate lighting isn't perfectly tuned for a real-time environment. Each method has its advantages and disadvantages. As a game artist, you have to make the right choices to achieve the effect that your game requires.

As you are aware from the previous chapter, lighting is an intensive process. Creating believable and realistic lighting takes not only the right technology, but also an artist's eye and skill. When lighting for games, it's necessary to master the tools at hand in order to pull off the look and feel you envision. Trying to re-create real-world lighting in games takes a combination of smart decisions and aesthetic knowledge. This chapter will discuss several of the common methods used to create real-time lighting for games. We'll start with the most frequently used solution, vertex lighting.

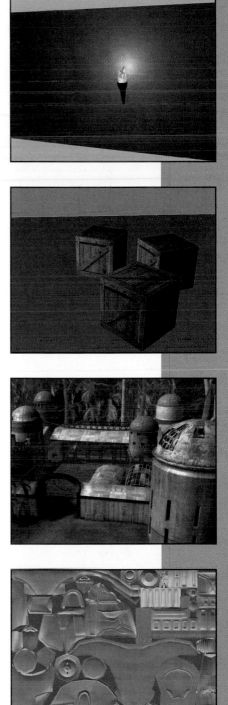

VERTEX LIGHTING

Vertex lighting is a technique that involves using the lights in a scene to color the vertices of the in-game geometry. This effectively "burns in" the lighting to the geometry, which is much less computationally expensive than calculating it on a per-pixel basis with real-time lights. In order to fully understand this concept, it might be helpful to first explore the concept of vertex color.

VERTEX COLOR

Most 3D packages and game engines support vertex color. When working with these packages and engines, every vertex in your scene has a color associated with it. The reason you don't see the color is because, by default, it is neutral gray (128, 128, 128) (in 3ds max it's white, 255, 255, 255). Until you actually assign a new color to a vertex and ask the 3D software to display the colors, you won't see a difference. Let me explain.

Figure 8.1 shows a simple triangle with three vertices, one on each corner.

To show you how vertex color works, let's assign colors to each of the vertices. I've given the top corner a red color (see Figure 8.2).

Now I'll set the bottom vertex color to blue. Notice the transition between the two vertices, giving us a violet hue in the middle (see Figure 8.3).

8.1 One triangle (or poly) with three vertices.

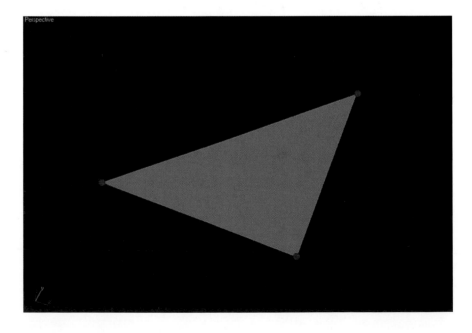

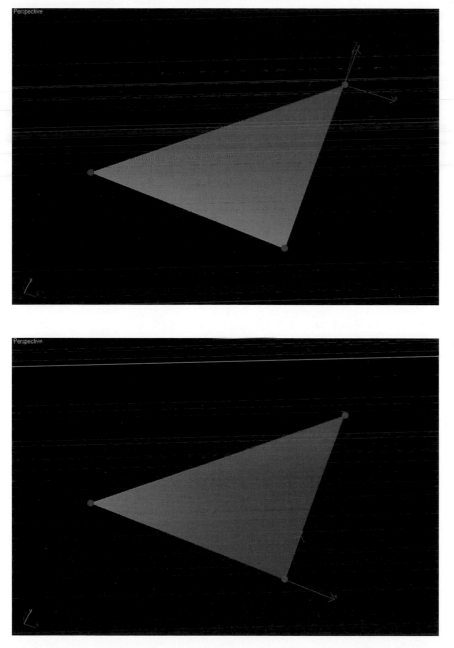

8.2 Each vertex can have its own color. Here I've assigned a red value to the upper vertex.

8.3 The bottom vertex is now blue. Notice the gradient between the two colored vertices.

Now I'll assign a green color to the remaining vertex. You can see that because each vertex is a different color, a gradient fade sweeps from one vertex to the next, blending between the colors (see Figure 8.4).

Think about vertex color this way: You are essentially burning color into your model's geometry. When your model is textured, the vertex color is multiplied on top of the texture. Multiplying is the most common

8.4 Each vertex with its own individual color assigned.

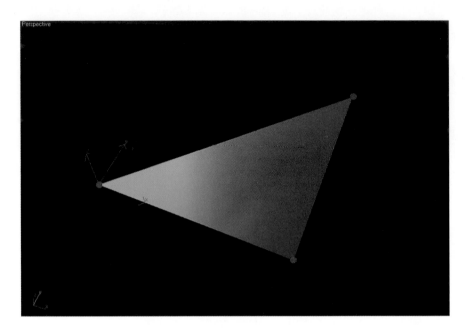

mode. In this case, the vertex color is similar to laying a piece of colored cellophane over the texture. The RGB values of each vertex color is multiplied by the RGB values in the texture.

In 3ds max, select a vertex, and at the bottom under the Modify tab, you'll see the options for vertex color (see Figure 8.5).

In addition, you have to go to the Properties of that object, check the Vertex Color box, and click on the Shaded button (see Figure 8.6).

8.5 Edit Vertex Colors under 3ds max's Modify panel.

Edit Vertex Colors

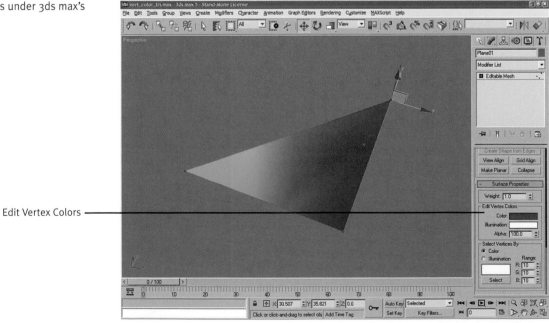

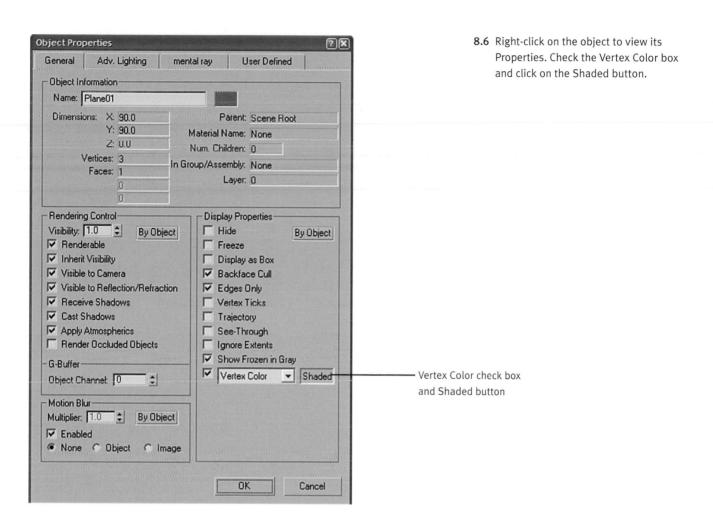

8.6 Right-click on the object to view its Properties. Check the Vertex Color box and click on the Shaded button.

Vertex Color check box and Shaded button

In Maya you go to Edit Polygons>Color>Apply Color. Once you assign vertex color in Maya, the display will automatically change so you can see the colors. Also, notice this command offers the option to Replace, Add, Subtract, or Remove the vertex color (see Figure 8.7).

To toggle vertex color display mode in Maya, with the object selected, go to Display>Custom Polygon Display and check the Color in Shaded Display check box on or off (see Figure 8.8).

Vertex color is pretty straightforward right? But what purposes does it serve? You'll be surprised at how powerful vertex coloring can be and how many potential uses there are for it. Let's take a look at a few uses in the following sections.

TIP

I typically make shelf buttons in Maya to toggle this on and off.

8.7 Applying color in Maya.

Color in Shaded Display
check box

8.8 The Color in Shaded Display check box in Maya.

VERTEX ALPHA

You'll notice that along with the option to change a vertex's color, you have the option to change the vert's alpha as well. This can be a powerful tool. You can make an object transparent without using a texture at all. It's much cheaper than a texture, and easy to use. Try to take advantage of this option as often as possible. Keep it in the back of your mind while you are texturing: Wait, do I need a 32-bit alpha texture? Or can I just use vertex alpha? In many cases, you can get away with not using a texture at all, just vertex color and alpha to get the desired result! But keep in mind, even though using vertex alpha is less expensive than an alpha texture, nothing is free, so talk with your programmers to find out how crazy you can go. Figure 8.9 shows a drinking glass with no texture or material at all. What you see was done by using vertex color and vertex alpha.

Another visual trick that can come in handy is to use a very slight bit of transparency to simulate a reflective material. Reflection maps work because they create the illusion that the environment around them is reflected in the material. In many cases, adding a slight transparency will allow colors and shapes of the surrounding environment to appear in the model, suggesting a shinier, more reflective surface. You can see this effect on the glass.

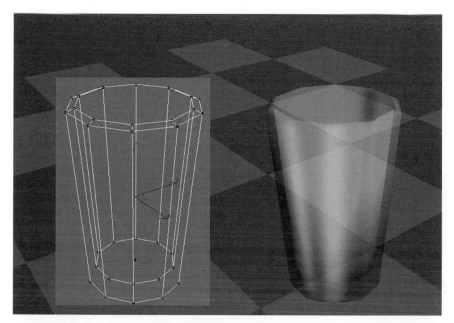

8.9 A glass created using only vertex color and vertex alpha. No texture necessary.

HIDING REPETITION

Use color to break up repetition and add more depth. Let's say you have a long brick wall with a tiled and repeated texture, as in Figure 8.10.

By changing the color of certain verts, you can minimize the obvious repetition by varying the colors along the wall and mixing up the values on the surface (see Figure 8.11).

8.10 Tiled and repeated texture.

8.11 Using vertex color to vary color values along the wall.

REUSING TEXTURES

You can use vertex color to create different color versions of the same texture as opposed to creating a whole new bitmap. Say you are creating a pile of multicolored computer diskettes. You could make six different textures, each a particular color. Or you can use one simple grayscale texture and use vertex color to change it up. This is a clear advantage in texture memory resources and good old-fashioned work savings. Take a look at Figures 8.12 and 8.13.

8.12 A grayscale diskette texture.

8.13 Using vertex color to get varying hues from the same texture.

UNDERSTANDING VERTEX LIGHTING

Now that you have an understanding of vertex color and how it works, we can apply that knowledge to vertex lighting. For many, vertex lighting is one of the most difficult-to-grasp concepts in creating 3D game art. So, what is vertex lighting? Well, we just learned how to manually change the colors of vertices. Vertex lighting is exactly that, except it uses the lights you place in 3D to color your verts. The trick is to not confuse this with typical lighting in 3D. You are not lighting your scene with lights; you are *using lights to color your vertices*. The resulting effect will always be slightly different than what you see in your viewport or render. The idea of vertex lighting is to *burn* the lighting information into the geometry itself. Remember how a game engine works—everything costs memory, and having real-time lights casting on your geometry on a per-pixel basis like a real render is a very expensive process. As I mentioned earlier, every vertex already has color information (it's just as simple as an RGB value associated with each vertex) and this is very inexpensive to the game engine. So if we can use the vertex color to create the illusion that the surfaces are being lit by lights, we save a ton of memory! Memory aside, this lighting method has several other advantages.

So now you have an idea of how to manually apply color to the vertices that make up a scene. Vertex lighting accomplishes the same thing—applying color to vertices—except that instead of you manually setting the color of each vertex, the color is set by the lights in your scene.

This is actually very different from the lighting methods we described in the previous chapter, where we created lights and the 3D renderer calculated the effects on a per-pixel basis. Those methods are generally too computationally demanding to use in real-time game engines. Vertex lighting instead takes advantage of the fact that the vertices in the scene all contain color information to begin with. The lighting effects are nearly free in terms of memory and processor usage.

Vertex lighting uses the distance, intensity, and color of the lights you place in your 3D scene to assign vertex colors to your geometry, creating the illusion that your objects are lit, and then burns the lighting information into your geometry.

In the following example, I've placed three lights of equal intensity—one red, one blue, and one green—near each vertex of the triangle. When I assign vertex colors to the geometry, it looks at the lights in my scene and chooses vertex colors based on the lighting information that exists (see Figure 8.14).

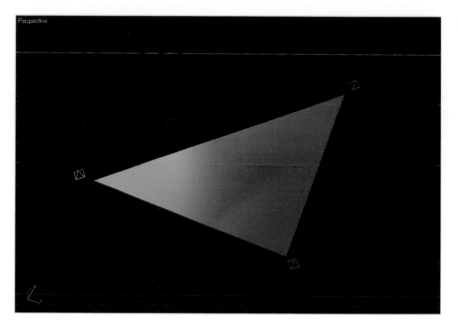

8.14 A tri with vertex colors assigned using lights.

Let's apply this to a typical lighting situation. In Figure 8.15 we have a plane with 10 subdivisions in each direction.

Now, I want to create a spotlight and cast a circle of light onto the plane from above. If I assign vertex colors now, we get the result shown in Figure 8.16.

Why does it look so bad? Here's the catch: The fewer vertices you have to work with, the less accurate the vertex lighting can be. In order to get a more accurate representation of the spotlight, we need to increase the

8.15 A plane with 10 subdivisions in each direction.

8.16 The plane with vertex lighting applied from a spotlight.

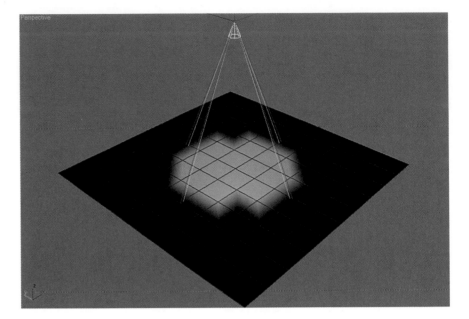

number of vertices on the plane. Let's change the subdivisions to 30 in each direction and see what happens (see Figure 8.17).

Much better. So this is the important lesson to be learned with vertex lighting. It's a bit of a catch-22. Vertex lighting is a cheap way to simulate lighting; on the other hand, you need more vertices to get a good result. In most situations you can get away with a few vertices. Think back to Chapter 3, where we discussed texture resolution and the importance of keeping it consistent. The same holds true for vertex resolution: A consistent mesh makes for more consistent lighting! Take a look at the crates shown in Figure 8.18.

8.17 The plane with increased subdivisions yields a more desirable result.

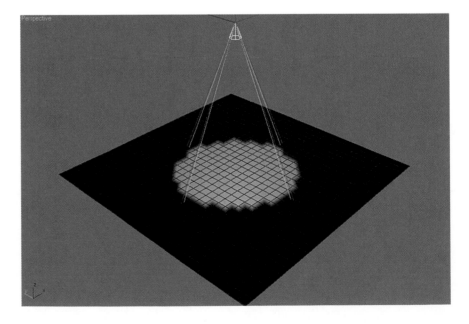

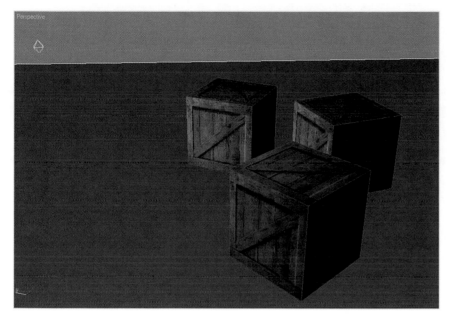

8.18 Crates with vertex lighting assigned.

This effect is very simple with a minimal amount of verts, but we get what we expect because all we need is flat lighting for each side.

To assign vertex color based on lighting in 3ds max, go to the Utilities tab and click the More button. This will bring up a list that contains Assign Vertex Colors. Open this rollout and, with your geometry selected, click the Assign to Selected button (see Figure 8.19).

In Maya, assigning vertex lighting is termed "Prelighting" because the method is also used to preview lighting without a render in high resolution geometry. Choose Edit Polygons>Color>Prelight (see Figure 8.20).

In theory, if you had an unlimited amount of polygons and vertices to work with, you could burn all your lighting information perfectly, making it indistinguishable from a render. But that would take an incredible amount of vertices. And as we know all too well, there are still polygon limits. So we have to choose the areas where lighting is most important and increase the number of verts in order to get good-looking lighting.

8.19 Assigning vertex lighting in 3ds max.

8.20 Prelight is Maya's command to assign vertex lighting.

THINGS TO WATCH OUT FOR

If you remember from Chapter 2, "Modeling Theory," we talked about keeping your geometry as grid-like as possible, avoiding star-like faces and uneven tessellation. You can now see that if your verts are not in the right place, you can get very funky lighting. Figure 8.21 shows a torch casting light on a wall with consistent and grid-like verts. The same wall with unevenly distributed vertices is shown in Figure 8.22.

As you can see, vertex lighting is a great solution if your lights are going to remain static and not move across the geometry. In Figure 8.23 you'll see a scene from *Medal of Honor*™. All the lighting in the game was done with vertex color.

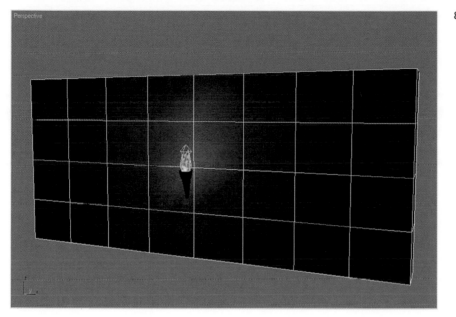

8.21 A vertex-lit wall with grid-like and clean geometry.

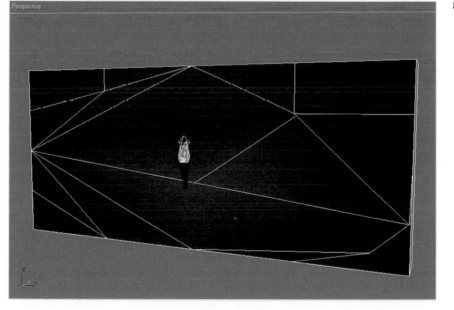

8.22 Unevenly distributed vertices cause major issues with vertex lighting.

8.23 A vertex-lit scene from *Medal of Honor Frontline*™.

Soft and Hard Edges

Another aspect of vertex lighting to keep in mind is that of soft and hard edges. Your vertices will color differently depending on the angle of your vertex normals. Figure 8.24 presents an example of a vertex-colored cylinder with hard edges. Figure 8.25 shows the same cylinder lit with soft edges.

8.24 A cylinder lit with hard edges.

Notice how the faces seem harsh and flat in Figure 8.24 as opposed to the smooth look of the same cylinder with smoothed edges. The light falls across the geometry in dramatically different ways. This is a powerful tool for modeling and lighting. Keep this in mind when you are lighting your objects.

When using vertex lighting, it's extremely important to keep your geometry stable by always deleting history and freezing transformations. Vertex lighting can be very finicky when objects have history or are not collapsed. I always get in the habit of deleting history, freezing transforms, and centering pivots of all the objects in my scene before I pre-light. Also note that there is different terminology for these steps across software applications. For example, in 3ds max, Freeze Transforms is called Reset Transforms, and Deleting History is called Collapsing.

LIGHTMAPS

Lightmaps or shadowmaps (you may also hear the terms texture baking, light baking, or render to texture) are one of the most accurate lighting solutions available for games. However, they can be considerably more expensive than vertex lighting. A lightmap is essentially a bitmap, like all other textures that you apply to your geometry.

A lightmap essentially looks at what the rendered image would be and creates a snapshot of the surface being lit. Based on that snapshot, it generates a new composite texture and reapplies it to the model. Other methods generate a new bitmap with alpha transparency that is overlayed across the geometry, sharing the same UV coordinates to represent the lighting effect on the surface.

The reason that lightmaps are so expensive is because you are potentially doubling the amount of textures in your scene, not to mention the fact that they are typically 32-bit textures with an alpha channel, which consumes more memory. But, if you need absolutely accurate lighting, lightmaps are a great choice. A lightmap stores the lighting information for the object in a separate map that is replaced or combined (multiplied) with the texture to provide a lit surface. Figures 8.26 through 8.28 show the elements of a lightmap.

You can see how each side of the cube is remapped with its new baked lighting texture. Lightmaps do a fantastic job of burning in lighting and shadow information, but increase the number of textures in your scene considerably. So use them wisely and sparingly.

8.26 The wall being lit by a torch.

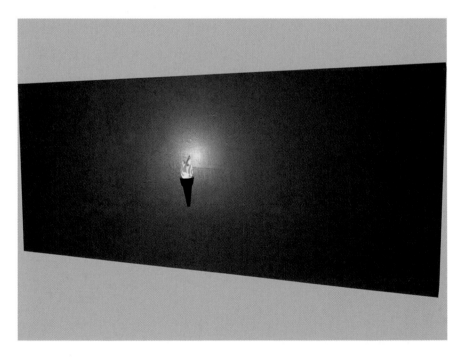

8.27 The wall's original texture.

8.28 The lightmap generated for the wall and reapplied with new UV coordinates.

PER-PIXEL LIGHTING

Per-pixel lighting is essentially the same concept as vertex lighting except that instead of coloring each vertex, the process colors each pixel. It should be obvious that this is a very accurate solution, and along with that comes the assumption that it is expensive in terms of both memory and processor consumption. That assumption is correct.

A pixel is the smallest unit that can be displayed on a screen. By bringing calculations for operations such as lighting and shading down to the smallest unit, developers can control such effects to the nth degree, making every image look great and as near a prerendered image as possible. Per-pixel lighting is currently limited to certain video cards and processors, but as the efficiency increases and hardware support becomes more widespread, you'll see per-pixel lighting and shading become the most effective lighting solution available. Figure 8.29 shows per-pixel lighting, nearly indistinguishable from a render.

8.29 Per-pixel lighting.

NORMAL MAPS

Normal mapping is an amazing and creative lighting solution used in some of today's most advanced games. The idea is quite similar to bump mapping, but is much more accurate and powerful. Normal mapping is being used more and more frequently in visually advanced games such as *Half Life 2* and *Doom 3*. Normal map generation tracks the surface normals of a high-poly model, and encodes that high-detail normal information to every pixel in the normal map for use on a low-poly mesh. So when light falls across the object, it appears to be extremely high in detail. Think of it as an invisible, high-detail shell around the low-poly object used to provide lighting information. If you remember how a bump map works, the concept is quite similar, except that we can now use three pieces of color information (RGB) as opposed to two (black and white). Bump maps use grayscale information to determine height. Normal maps use RGB values to provide X, Y, and Z information to calculate lighting and surface properties, giving a more realistic and believable illusion. Just as LOD or proxies allowed the swapping in of lower- or higher-poly models based on viewing distance, normal mapping allows the use of lighting information from a much higher detailed model than the one actually used in the game. It is basically a real-time shader that takes bump mapping to the next level. When a light is shone across the surface, it creates the illusion that the geometry is much higher in detail than it really is.

If you haven't noticed by now, everything that is cool comes with a price. Normal mapping is no exception. The obvious downside to using normal maps is that for every object, an entirely new map is generated.

Normal maps typically do not have to be the same size as the texture. For example, say you have a texture on a rock wall that is 512×512. The Normal map for that wall could easily be 256×256.

OK, so we have cut the size in half, but add up all the objects in your scene and you'll find that it amounts to a considerable number of new files. That is why normal mapping is currently used sparingly and in conjunction with other lighting methods such as vertex and lightmaps. Most games that currently use normal mapping, use them for characters. The detail of characters is one of the most noticeable features in games. As humans ourselves, we quickly notice when things are not right. We know how we look, move, and act. Creating a character that is believable is a difficult task. Normal maps provide us with the lighting information we expect to see in a real-world situation. That's why normal maps are used primarily for characters and animals—because we can *feel* the reality.

Let's take a look at a normal mapping procedure. Figure 8.30 displays the torso of a droid that will be used in a game. We start with a game resolution model with minimal poly count.

8.30 The in-game model of a droid.

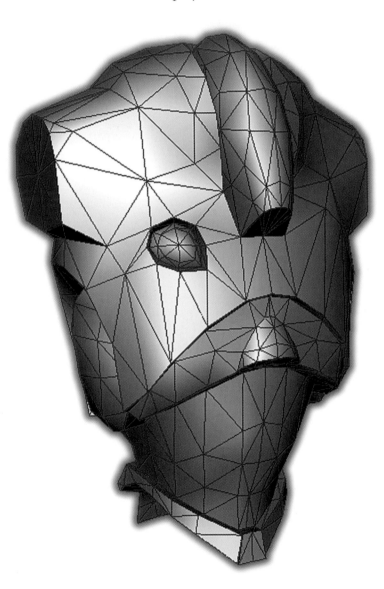

Once the final in-game model has been tested by the animators and we know it will not change, we can start to create a more detailed version of the model to use as the normal mapping geometry (see Figure 8.31).

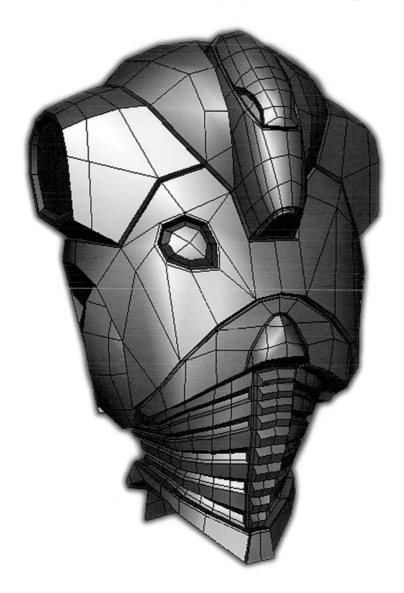

8.31 Adding details and smoothing the geometry.

One great trick in creating highly detailed normal maps is to convert to Subdivision Surfaces in order to define details and creases. SubD's "crease" command yields nice results. Figure 8.32 shows the droid converted to SubD and refined until we have a great-looking, high-res model from which to extract normal information.

8.32 The high-res model.

When building the high-res model, you should watch out for a couple
of potential problems:

- Avoid making extreme changes to the silhouette of your geometry.

- Avoid overlapping geometry or deep holes because they will cause
  the normal map to distort.

You can see the RGB values of the normal map and how they relate to
the model in Figure 8.33.

8.33 The RGB values associated with the
vertex normals.

Next, we take that lighting information and generate a map that will be assigned to the low-poly, in-game model (see Figure 8.34).

The final in-game model looks significantly more detailed than it really is, solely based on lighting information (see Figure 8.35).

8.34 The final normal map for the entire droid.

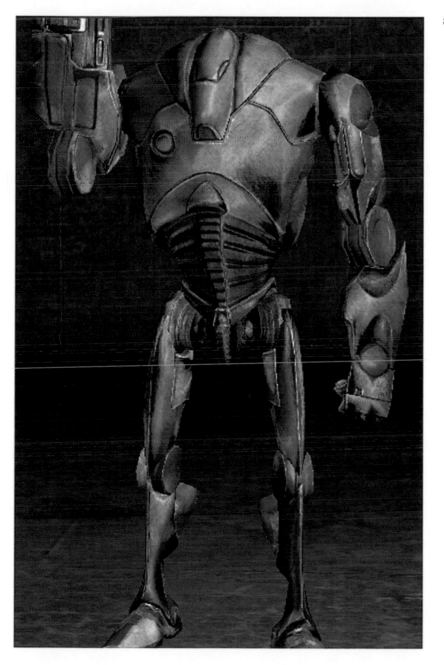

8.35 The final in-game model showing far more detail than is actually there, thanks to a normal map.

DYNAMIC LIGHTING

The term *dynamic lights* means one thing: animated light. When a torch flickers against a wall, or a swinging light bulb illuminates the scene around it as it moves, you are witnessing dynamic lighting. This effect can, of course, be achieved in many ways, most of which have been discussed already. It should be obvious to you by now that the only reason you don't see dynamic light everywhere in every game is because it is expensive. Take vertex lighting, for example. Even though we know vertex lighting can be one of the cheapest lighting procedures, animating vertex lighting changes things quite quickly. It's easy enough to burn in the color to a vertex, knowing it's not going to change. But when you need vertex colors to animate quickly, it's nearly as computationally intensive as animating an object moving through space.

Other examples of dynamic lighting you can see in today's games include explosions that briefly illuminate the surrounding area, time of day change, flashing or blinking lights, and lightning flashing across an environment.

Typically, dynamic lighting is done most efficiently and effectively using vertices. This is simply because, in most cases, dynamic lighting takes place very quickly. An oil barrel explodes; the quick flash you see doesn't have to be perfectly detailed. As long as the area surrounding the explosion illuminates, it happens so fast that it doesn't have to be precise and still has the same visual effect as if it were detailed.

TROUBLESHOOTING

Once you start lighting and exporting to a game engine, you can expect some issues to pop up with respect to lighting. Here are a few common problems to look for.

BLACK OR INVISIBLE FACES ON GEOMETRY

A solid black face or object is typically an issue with normals. Most of the time, you'll find the normals of a face have been reversed or the entire object's normals are inside out. This will often show up as invisible faces as well. Check your model and make sure all the normals are pointing in the right direction.

INCONSISTENCY

Another common issue that arises with vertex lighting is when faces that are connected do not display lighting information in the same way. It can be quite frustrating. Take a look at Figure 8.36.

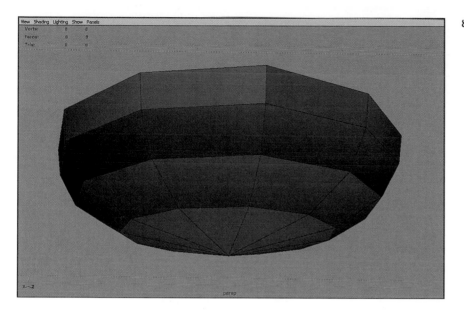

This is usually the first sign that you may have history on your object. 3D software packages have a hard time calculating vertex colors when the objects still have history associated with them. Remember to always delete history, freeze transforms, and center pivots to ensure you have the cleanest geometry possible. This can also happen with mismanaged smoothing groups or inconsistent vertex normals.

Blown Out or Overexposed Lighting

Often when lighting, you may find that your scene suddenly becomes what may appear over-bright and washed out. Keep in mind that the brightness of lights tends to increase exponentially. The more lights you add to your scene, the higher the overall intensity in the scene. Check for ambient lights or lights that have no decay. It's best to use as few lights as possible to achieve the desired effect in your scene. Fewer lights also helps when managing and organizing your lights.

Conclusion

Lighting for games takes some time and practice, but when you get it right, your scene will look professional and realistic. With all the lighting solutions that are available, it can be a challenging decision as to what will work best for your game. In the most recent games, all these techniques are used in combination. Again, we come back to making intelligent and creative decisions. That is what makes this so fun! Knowing the advantages and disadvantages is the first step to deciding what is best for your game. In the next chapter, we'll discuss effects and how they can add life and atmosphere to your scene.

9

EFFECTS

AS YOU HAVE SEEN, dealing with a real-time environment calls for some ingenuity. Realistic and convincing effects pose one of the greatest challenges yet.

Whether it's fog, rain, or explosions, creating effects for display in real-time takes some creative problem solving. Before we focus on effects for games, I'd like to talk a bit about prerendered effects in order to provide a proper comparison.

Traditional CG effects can be generated in numerous ways. Much of what you see in feature films or commercials is prerendered, or composited in postproduction. Adobe After Effects is a popular compositing program that can be used to create and combine effects of all kinds. This process is different from real-time in that with prerendered images, you can layer, animate, blend, and apply filters, and then put it all together into one final rendered movie. We're not quite there yet in the real-time world, but it won't be long! As it is, we can still do some very neat stuff (see Figure 9.1).

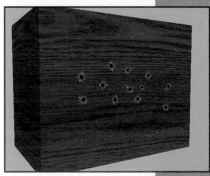

With games, we don't have the luxury of a true postproduction process. Most everything we see on the screen is happening in real-time

and running at 30 to 60 frames per second. The advances that are being made with respect to multi-pass rendering, programmable shaders, and frame buffer effects are truly impressive, but until these features become mainstream, we need more efficient and creative solutions.

There are a lot of interesting and creative ways to create complex effects in a real-time environment. Particle systems, animated and camera-facing billboards, vertex fogging, and dynamic lighting are all great examples of effects. Of course, the goal remains the same: to get the effect you want, and at the same time keep the memory imprint small. Let's discuss a few of the options.

Particle Effects

Particle effects (or systems) are exactly what they sound like: a grouping of small particles, either 3D geometry or camera-facing sprites, that are emitted from a specific object or location in the world.

Unlike traditional 3D software package particles, game effects are typically 2D sprites or point sprites, which are similar to simple two-poly squares except you cannot manipulate vertices or select individual sprites. Each point sprite has a small texture and alpha channel, and is emitted from a certain point and affected by forces like lifetime, velocity, and gravity.

Figure 9.2 shows a few frames from a simple water fountain effect created using only one texture and a few straightforward parameters.

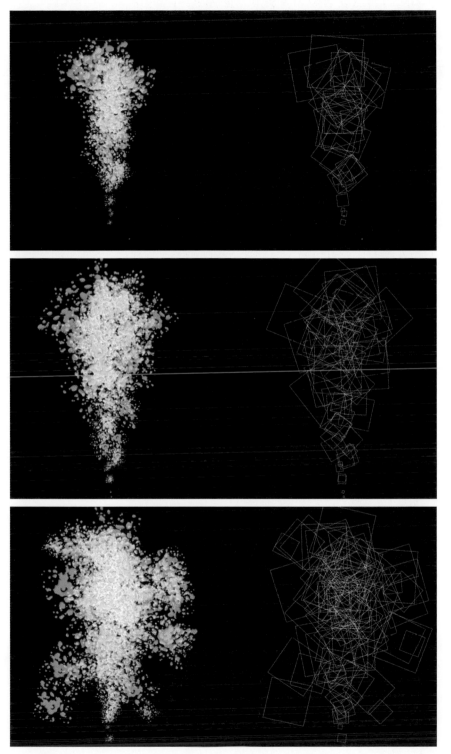

9.2 A sequence of frames from a camera-facing sprite fountain effect.

You can clearly see that fairly small, flat, low-poly sprites can convincingly create the illusion of 3D particles. Notice that the sprites always face the camera, giving the effect of depth and volume. And when a character happens to walk around this effect, the sprites will always be facing the player's point of view, which does a nice job of simulating 3D objects in space as long as they are smaller objects and not overused. There is still no substitute for real 3D geometry, however. You can clearly see this if you open one of the files you downloaded from the web site, fountain_rotate.AVI. The texture is a 32×32 TGA, with an alpha channel for transparency (see Figure 9.3).

9.3 A water texture with alpha.

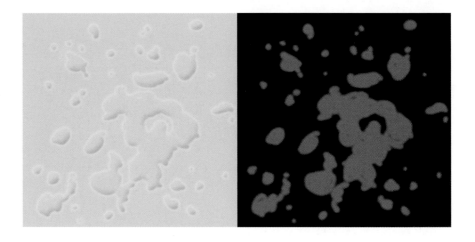

TEXTURES FOR EFFECTS

When it comes to textures for effects, obviously the rule is the smaller, the better. Textures for sprites typically range anywhere from 8×8 to 256×256 pixels. The size you choose depends on the same principles used when deciding how to texture your scene. Think about these factors:

- Size—The physical size of the particle.

- Distance—How close the camera will get to an individual sprite.

A good comparison would be between a raindrop and a fireball for a large explosion. The raindrop will always be a small sprite and not take up much of the screen. The entire rain effect may take up a lot of the screen, and there will most likely be a lot of these sprites. All the more reason to keep the texture small. We could easily get away with an 8×8 size for this texture (see Figure 9.4).

The explosion, on the other hand, could potentially be right in front of the camera, and is a large effect. I'd use at least a 128×128 size, preferably a 256×256 one (see Figure 9.5).

Although some companies use 3D software packages such as 3ds max, Maya, or Houdini to generate particle effects for their games, it is more common for game companies to have their own proprietary software that is specifically designed for exporting effects to their game engine. Whether you are using 3ds max or a proprietary package, you'll find that aside from terminology and special features, the basic elements and parameters for creating particles will be the same.

An effect typically consists of one or more emitters. Emitters are the points of origin of a particle effect, whether it's a point in space, an object, or sometimes even a particle itself.

The following lists some common parameters you can expect to work with, along with explanations of their functionality. Again, terminology typically varies from software to software, so you'll find some alternate terms in parentheses.

- Emitter—Choose the type of emitter you want your particle to spawn from: a cube, a sphere, a point, or a character weapon. Often, models are built with effect hard points. Basically, these are dummy objects or locators that serve as a point from which an effect will emit. In the example of the fountain, the particles are being spawned from a small planar emitter.

- Texture— Lets you specify which texture will be used on the particle. A texture can be projected onto each individual sprite (face mapping), or spread across the entire effect. Each sprite in the fountain effect is face mapped.

- Life (Lifespan)—The amount of time an individual particle will stay on screen after being spawned. If you choose one second as life, the particle will spawn, do its thing, and die off after one second.

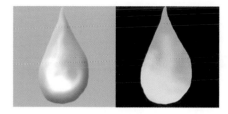

9.4 A raindrop sprite. An 8x8 texture will work great.

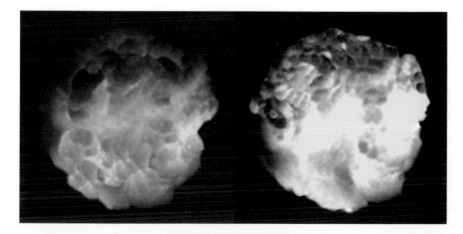

9.5 The explosion sprite needs to be quite a bit larger, 256×256.

- Velocity (Speed)—The speed at which a particle travels when spawned from the emitter. The higher the number, the higher the traveling speed of the particle will be, and the longer it will take for gravity to affect it.

- Rate—The number of particles that will be generated. Inputting "1" will give you one sprite. Always try to use the smallest number possible that will still achieve the desired look.

- Color Start and End (RBG)—Just like it sounds, you set the RGB values for the beginning and end. The colors will change over the lifetime of the effect. Alpha transparency is typically included with this option. It lets you define the start and end opacity of the particles. Rising smoke is a good example of opacity: The smoke may start off black and fairly dense, but as it rises to the sky, the color may become lighter and the opacity will reduce as the smoke dissipates.

- Spread (Direction)—This lets you choose the angle and direction in which the particles are emitted. Using the fountain as an example, the spread would cause the particles to move outward from the origin and gives us the cone/spray shape as opposed to a straight line of particles.

- Particle Size—Similar to color, this lets you set the start size and end size; the effect will interpolate between the two. The fountain particles start small and end at three times their original size. This adds to the spreading and spray effect, giving the fountain more density towards the end.

- Gravity (Force)—Lets you set whether gravity affects the particles, and if so, how much. In the fountain example, gravity is what would cause the water to fall back to earth after their velocity has worn itself out. The fountain is emitting particles upward, but with gravity applied to the effect, the particles fall back down to earth at a particular point. Think of gravity as fighting against velocity.

- Position (Offset)—Allows you to tweak where the effect spawns without moving your emitter or hard point. Handy for subtle adjustments.

- Rotation (Spin)—Even though many of the sprites in an effect are camera-facing, they can still rotate in one axis. This adds an important amount of realism to particle systems. Imagine bullet casings flying out of a gun with no rotation on them; you'd get something unnatural rather than a realistic movement. Rotation also helps to create a more dynamic and organic effect by providing more movement and random overlap. In the fountain example (see fountain.AVI from the book's web site), you can see the effect rotation has on motion.

- Mode. Rendering Modes Additive = (particle RGB + background RGB), Multiplicative = (particle RGB × background RGB), and Subtractive = (particle RGB − background RGB)—This option allows you to choose different rendering modes. Using this parameter can be beneficial for many reasons. Additive can be used to give explosions a more blown-out look, or can make an effect show up better in a night scene.

- Bias—Most of these parameters will have a bias or min/max value associated with them. If you want more color variation in your effect, you could set the Minimum RGB value to 237, 239, 255, and the Maximum value to 77, 92, 232. This means that when your particles emit, the color they are "born" with could randomly be anywhere between these values. You'll also hear terms like randomize or jitter, which serve a similar purpose.

More advanced particle generation systems are already being used in recent games. It won't be long before the majority of the restrictions we currently face will be history. You'll have all the power you could want to create the perfect effects. Some features that were typically limited to prerendered effects that are already becoming common today are:

- Instanced geometry—No more sprites. You can effectively select any 3D model and use it as the emitted particle.

- Inter-particle collision—Dynamic particles that bounce off the ground, walls, and even each other.

- Bezier curves—Instead of the values changing linearly between particle birth and death, we can specify values at different time offsets during the particle's life, which are then interpolated smoothly using Bezier curves, affecting color, rotation, and other aspects of each particle's behavior during its lifetime.

- Per-particle emitters—Each individual particle can act as an emitter. For example, a flying piece of debris could have a flaming particle attached to it.

> **EFFECTS AND MEMORY**
>
> As you can probably guess, even though we are using small sprites as opposed to 3D geometry, effects can still be quite the memory hogs. Think about a scene filled with smoke, fire, explosions, and the like. There are an awful lot of textures being displayed at one time. There are many situations where particles can slow down your frame rate significantly. One is, of course, if you just have too many effects playing at the same time. More particles require more memory. More particles also take up a lot more CPU power because there are more of them to evaluate per frame. Also, the amount of the screen that is taken up by effects (pixel coverage) makes a big difference. For example, if you have only one effect playing, but the camera is extremely close to it, the screen will be filled with sprites. This can easily bog down an engine. So it's important to consider where your effects will be playing in relation to the camera.

BILLBOARDS

Billboards are similar to particle effects in that they are sprites that can face the camera. Billboards typically use larger textures (256×256 and up) and are usually static, aside from their rotation to face a camera. A sequence of billboards can also be used to play an animation. One of the most frequent uses for billboards is to give physical lights in a scene a glow or halo around them. This is a great effect to give a scene a sense of atmosphere (see Figures 9.6 and 9.7).

9.7 The billboards glow texture, 128×128.

9.6 A lightbulb with, and without, a glow billboard.

FOG

Fog can be created in several ways. The most common and efficient method to simulate fog is by using vertex color. In the previous chapter, we discussed why vertex lighting is such a cheap option. The same is true for creating fog. The engine will add color to all the vertices in your scene, adding more color towards the distance and less in the foreground, to create the impression of environmental fog. As an artist you can expect to have several parameters to work with when adding fog.

- Fog Start and End distances (or fog clipping planes)—Imagine two walls that contain the fog between them (see Figure 9.8). The closer together you move the walls, the more dense the fog gets. The farther apart, the more thinned out it becomes (see Figure 9.9).

- Fog Density (or Intensity)—Lets you set how strong or dense the fog is between the clipping planes.

- Fog Color—Lets you specify a color for the fog. It's best to have control over the near color and far color if you can talk your programmer into it.

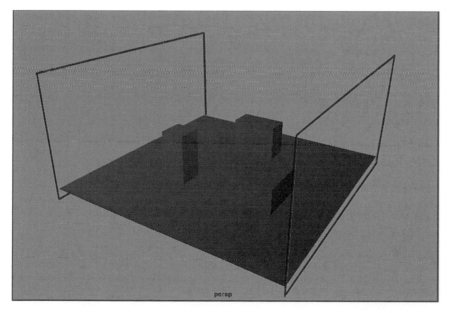

9.8 Fog between two planes.

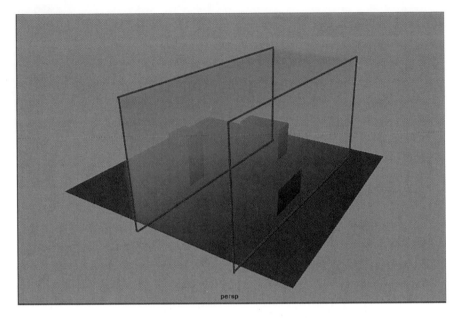

persp

The vertex color method works well for establishing distance and giving your scene some depth, but what if you need more realistic volumetric fog? There are other options for creating believable fog.

- Particle Fog—Just like it sounds, you create a particle system that simulates moving fog in your scene. This is obviously more costly with respect to memory.

- Billboard Fog Effects—Using camera-facing billboards to simulate volume. See the section on clouds later in this chapter. The same process works well for volume fog, but is a costly choice due to the fact that they are nearly full-screen alpha blends.

WATER

Making realistic water can be quite difficult, particularly when you have only so much memory to work with. Depending on the type of water you want, it can be simple, or very complex. A small pond or pool of water that is static and not moving is quite easy. Simple alpha transparency and a nice texture can give you the result you are looking for. But a large ocean, with turbulent waves and moving specularity, is a different story altogether.

One of the best methods to use when making puddles and small bodies of static standing water is a simple plane with a subtle texture, alpha transparency, and mirrored geometry to simulate reflection (see Chapter 11, "User Interface Design and Creation").

Making a convincing ocean can be a complicated endeavor. Traditional CG uses displacement, bump, and specularity to achieve realism. If your game engine supports any of these features, you'll be in pretty good shape. Without them, you have to get creative.

One commonly used method is to use two transparent textures with UVs that slide in alternate directions or at different speeds (scrolling UVs). This will give the water some depth and movement. You can see this method used widely in games like *Secret Weapons over Normandy* (see Figure 9.10) or *Jedi Starfighter*.

Another option that can give water more movement and detail is a combination of a base texture and a sequence of tiled, animated frames playing over the top. This is a great way to simulate deformed CG water. You can use 3ds max or Maya to create high-resolution water with deformations, specular highlights, and realistic motion. Render out a sequence of frames from the top view, make sure they are tilable and that the animation is looped, and you have the frames you need to make some great-looking water (see Figure 9.11).

This method does have some negatives. One is that when seen from above, the water looks great, but if you look at it from a low angle, you'll notice it is still flat. Another flaw is the risk of repetition. Whenever you tile a texture over a large flat surface, you will likely see the repeating pattern. The base texture can do a good job of breaking up the repetition if your tiled layer has enough transparency.

9.10 Scrolling water planes in *Secret Weapons over Normandy.*

9.11 A sequence of animated, tilable, looping water frames.

Another effective method is Color Vertex Cycling (CVC). Basically, CVC is animating the colors of vertices over time. This is more costly than static vertex color but can give you color change and a sense of motion. CVC is commonly used to create motion in rivers and oceans. It is also useful for creating more variation in color over large bodies of water.

The reflection and refraction of the sun or moon on the surface of an ocean is an important aspect of creating believable water. This can also be done in a few ways. Of course, the preferred method would be real specularity based on deformed geometry and position of the sun. But since that is quite pricey, we have to get creative again. The most common solution is enacted by using our good old friend, vertex color. Because the reflection moves across the water, it is technically CVC that is taking place. This also assumes that there are enough vertices on the water plane to work with.

Another option is to create a large texture with transparency that sits on top of and moves along the water plane. However, it's more expensive than vertex color in terms of memory and processor usage, and unless done properly, can look wrong and out of place.

CLOUDS

Clouds can be created as either a particle system or camera-facing billboards. Billboards are typically the preferred method because they are cheap and effective in terms of memory and processor usage. Figures 9.12 and 9.13 illustrate how cloud billboards might be oriented in order to create the illusion of volume.

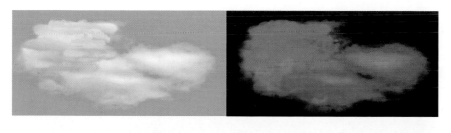

9.12 The cloud texture at 256×128.

9.13 You can see how a few simple camera-facing billboards can produce the illusion of volume.

DECALS

Decals are small sprites that sit on top of geometry like a sticker. The use of decals varies, from signage to bullet impacts. In *Medal of Honor*™, as well as many other action games, decals are used to simulate bullet impacts and blast marks on different surfaces. As you would imagine for bullet impacts, the textures do not have to be very large. A 16×16 or 32×32 texture will work well in most cases (see Figure 9.14). A good impact system will have random size and rotation, giving the impacts more of a varied and organic look. Let's look at an example of decals generated on impact with random rotation and size (see Figure 9.15).

You can see what a great concept using small sprites to simulate impact is. It's effective and quite straightforward. Notice that the texture maintains some transparency, which allows the colors of the objects behind it to blend, helping the decal look more in place on different surfaces. Adding the random rotation and scaling helps keep the impact looking more organic and natural.

9.14 The decal texture, with alpha at 32×32.

9.15 Sprites floating on the surface.

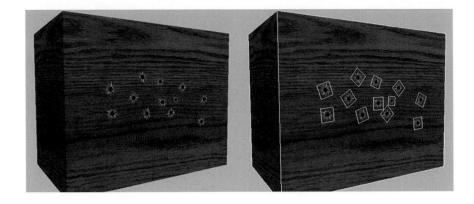

CONCLUSION

Finding creative ways to give your scene life with effects can be a rewarding process. Studying the examples shown in this chapter, I'm sure you can imagine thousands of uses for these concepts. Remember that there is always opportunity to come up with your own solutions and methods. Keep an open mind when you are working on a project, and you'll be surprised at how many new ideas are just waiting to be realized.

[CHAPTER] 10

TIPS AND TRICKS

THIS CHAPTER IS MEANT TO offer you some of the tricks, tips, and
shortcuts I have picked up over the years while making games. All
of the ideas presented here are focused on helping you take your
work to the next level. You've heard me preach about setting a new
standard for yourself and continually raising your own personal
quality bar. I am hoping that the information and methods offered
to you in this book so far have already enabled you to think a bit
differently about how you approach 3D. The ideas in this chapter
attempt to carry on that inspiration and offer some more detailed
and specific examples that will continue to spark your most creative
thoughts and approaches.

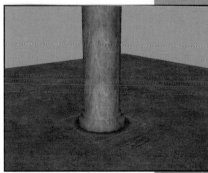

Chapter 3, "Introduction to Texturing," presented the idea of invest-
ing that extra time and creativity to make your textures more interesting and realistic. Now, I'd like to get into some specific techniques
I use to create that *extra something* in your models and textures. Many
of the ideas I'll demonstrate here can be applied to a limitless number of situations, so the best thing I can do for you is to offer you
some ways of working that will enable you to approach your workflow in a different way.

THE METAL BOX

I'm going to try to show you several tricks for taking your textures to the next level by using a simple example of a metal box. We'll work through the process of taking a basic metal texture and, using only Photoshop, creating a more interesting and realistic texture.

So, imagine our job is to model and texture a metal box. Modeling it is pretty easy, and slapping a metal texture on the box is easy. So let's start there. Figure 10.1 shows the box and the metal texture.

All right, metal box done, right? Not on my watch. Sure, it looks like a metal box, but we can definitely improve on it. In Chapter 4, "Advanced Texturing," we talked about the power of using layers in Photoshop. When I'm painting textures, I typically add what I call a grunge layer. Its purpose is to break up the flatness of the surface and add some depth and variation. To create the new layer, I take a large, soft-edged paintbrush and a dark color (close to black), and paint some simple strokes across the image. Take a look at Figure 10.2.

Next, I bring down the opacity of that layer until it is subtle enough, but still makes a visual difference (see Figure 10.3).

Now, just like we saw in Chapter 4, I'm going to copy and paste a new metal layer from my texture library on top to add a bit of color and some character. I brought the opacity of this layer down to 31% (see Figure 10.4).

10.1 The metal texture assigned to the box.

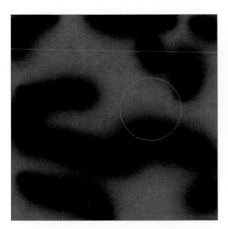

10.2 Painting a new grunge layer that gives the image more depth and variation.

10.3 Adjusting the opacity of the layer until you get the desired result.

10.4 Adding another metal layer to bring in color and add more depth.

Next, I want to show you a trick that I have found works very well for helping establish surface characteristics. I'm going to add (on a new layer, of course) a soft white border around the image by using a soft paintbrush and holding down the Shift key (which locks your stroke in a horizontal or vertical position). (See Figure 10.5.)

I did this because I want to create the illusion that the edges of the box are more rounded and thick. Currently, the box looks like it is made out of thin, flimsy metal pieces that meet at perfect 90-degree angles. Not very realistic. Sure, we could add subdivisions and polys to the model to soften and round the edges, but I think you'll see how effectively you can pull this off by using this texture. Now, I'll bring down the opacity to about 24%, to keep it subtle. It is almost unnoticeable, but take a look at Figure 10.6 to see what happens when we update the texture on the box.

See how the edges now seem less rigid and more rounded? It even makes the metal look thicker and more realistic. The reason this works so well is because where the two edges meet, the brush stroke is most opaque; then the stroke fades off towards the center of the texture, creating the illusion that the edges are rounded. This works great for most surfaces, and it works particularly well in games, where hard edges are all too common!

OK, let's keep going. Next, I'm going to quickly use the eraser to remove parts of the white border, just to make it look more organic and less perfect. Remember, we are always trying to avoid the perfect computer-generated look. I'm also going to make sure not to erase anything on the absolute edge; otherwise, I'd be bringing back that stark edge. Figure 10.7 shows the updated texture.

10.5 Painting a soft white border around the edges of the texture.

10.6 You can see what a major difference adding that soft edge makes to the surface of the box.

10.7 Although the difference is subtle, notice how the edges seem more organic and not so perfect.

You can play another trick on the eye by using value change, suggesting that a surface is not as flat as it really is. By painting a subtle brightness or darkness in the center of the texture, you create the illusion that the metal is bulging outward or denting inward. Take a look at Figure 10.8. You can see how just a small change in the texture can affect how the surface of an object appears. Keep this in mind as you are painting textures.

10.8 Using lightness or darkness to suggest that the metal is denting inward or bulging outward.

Even though the box is starting to look better, there is still opportunity to take it even further. Let's do a few things to make the box look older and more used. We'll start by adding some scratches and small dents in areas that make sense. Here is where we need to stop and think again about the box; if it were beat up a bit more, where would the evidence of scratches or dings most likely be? Around the corners and along the edges seem to be the most likely places. I'm going to use a very subtle bevel and emboss to make the box look like it has been tossed around and banged into over time. This will give it character and a history (see Figure 10.9). At the same time, you have to be careful not to make the features too unique or stand out too much; otherwise, we'll notice repetition.

You'll also notice I added a soft brown-red outer glow to the scratches layer to suggest that the "wounds" are starting to rust. It also helps to add a bit of color to the image, adding to the depth.

10.9 Adding scratches and dents to give the box more character and suggest a history.

Speaking of color, what if this box were once painted? How could we convey that?

Another great trick I found in Photoshop is to use the Paint Bucket tool with the All Layers box (located in the top center) checked to simulate things like old peeling paint or chipped metal and wood. All kinds of organic flaws and markings can be painted quickly and easily with the Paint Bucket. The key is the All Layers check box. By default it is turned off, and when you fill a layer you get just what you'd expect: a total flood fill of the entire image. But with All Layers checked, and by adjusting the tolerance, the fill will actually sample the pixels in the image and fill only certain areas, depending on the contrast of the pixels. Imagine dripping small amounts of colored water onto a very coarse piece of sandpaper. The colored water would take the path of least resistance through the grains. The All Layers option works the same way. The pixels act as the sandpaper, and you can get some really amazing effects with this method. Take a look at Figure 10.10, where I added the look of old, peeled-away paint to the box.

To further enhance the effect, I added some noise to the paint layer to give it some variation, and also added a very subtle drop shadow to suggest that the paint has some thickness to it. In addition, I made a quick pass with the eraser to scratch the paint in certain areas.

I could go on and on with this exercise, but the intent was to show you some important tricks and tools that I have learned while painting textures. Hopefully, you can take these lessons and apply them to numerous situations you'll face in the future.

10.10 Using the Paint Bucket tool with All Layers checked to create the look of old, peeling paint.

TREES AND VEGETATION

Creating realistic trees, bushes, grass, and the like is one of the most difficult challenges a 3D artist can face. If you were to model every leaf and branch of a tree, you'd have quite a high poly model. As usual, we have to get creative. One of the most effective ways of generating vegetation for games is by taking full advantage of our old friend, the alpha channel. By using a combination of alpha and simple geometry, you'll be surprised at how realistic and detailed you can make a tree look without going poly-crazy. Let's use a pine tree as an example. For this pine tree, we are going to use only two small textures: a tilable bark texture (128×64) and a branch texture (256×256) with alpha (see Figure 10.11).

We'll start with the trunk of the tree. Create a cylinder (depending on the type of tree and complexity of your scene, you can easily get away with a five-sided or even three-sided cylinder with smooth vertex normals). This example has three sides. I'll remove the top and bottom faces because we know that the player will not see them (see Figure 10.12).

Now I'm going to assign the bark texture to the cylinder before I change its shape so I can lock in the UV coordinates. I'll tile it three times in Y (see Figure 10.13). Next, I'm going to scale down the top vertices to give the trunk its tapered form (see Figure 10.14).

10.11 The two textures we'll use to create the entire tree.

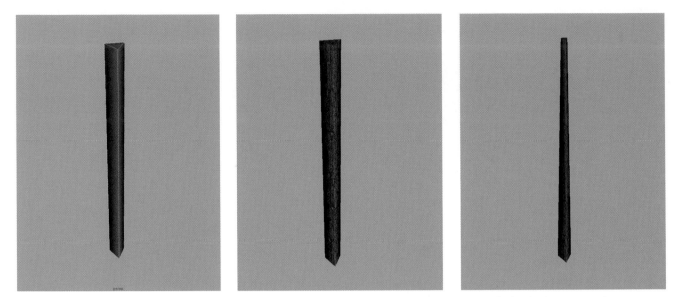

10.12 The basic three-sided pine tree trunk with smooth vertex normals.

10.13 The trunk with the tiled bark texture assigned.

10.14 The basic pine tree trunk.

Before we go any further, let's take a closer look at the texture we are going to use for the branches.

I've paid close attention to the alpha channel to make sure I'm getting the most out of it. Figure 10.15 shows the texture we will be using for the branches.

You can see there is a slight overall transparency to the branch leaves, but not the branch itself. Most vegetation is translucent, which means that light penetrates into a leaf and bounces around within the object, giving it not only semi-transparency, but also a subtle type of glow. Giving the needles a bit of transparency in the alpha helps create this illusion. I've also tried to match the colors of the background and the elements in the image to minimize any pixel bleeding. Notice also that I darkened the branch with a gradient towards the stem of the branch so that when these branches are layered on top of one another, the tree will appear denser.

To make the branch, create a rectangular-shaped plane that has one sub-division along its longer side (see Figure 10.16).

10.15 The branch texture and its alpha.

10.16 A plane with one subdivision will act as our branch.

Now, let's move the branch outward and move the pivot point to the center of the trunk. You'll see why this is a good idea momentarily. To move the pivot in Maya, hit the Insert key (see Figure 10.17). In 3ds max, in the Hierarchy panel, hit the Affect Pivot Only button.

Next, assign the texture and UVs (see Figure 10.18). Now let's move the plane vertically up the trunk. I also moved the individual vertices up and down to give the branch some depth (see Figure 10.19).

10.17 Moving the plane outward and the pivot to the center of the trunk.

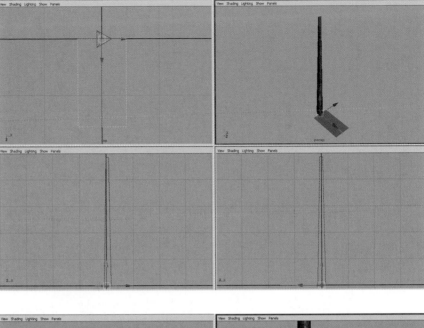

10.18 The branch texture with alpha assigned to the plane.

10.19 By translating the verts, a simple plane with alpha can make for a pretty convincing low-poly branch.

So now, let's fill in the rest of the tree. The reason we moved the pivot point of the branch to the center of the trunk is because we can now rotate and duplicate the branches with less effort. By duplicating the existing branch and rotating it around the trunk, we can quickly fill the tree. Just scale down the branches as you copy them upward toward the top of the tree (see Figure 10.20). Notice that for the top of the tree, I just used two simple quads with the same texture that intersect each other.

10.20 Duplicating, rotating, and scaling let you fill the entire tree with the same branch.

To duplicate almost any object or component in Maya, hit Ctrl+D. In 3ds max, hold down the Shift key before and while you click and translate.

Now we have a pine tree that is less than 160 polys! Perfect if you know you are going to have many of the trees in close proximity. Let's duplicate the tree and make a small grouping (see Figure 10.21). In order to make each tree look a bit different, scale and rotate the trees as you duplicate them.

> **TIP**
>
> To further differentiate them, manipulate the individual verts on each tree, or use a Lattice or FFD box to change the overall shape and make each one unique.

Now that we have a grouping, let's look at some efficient and creative ways to make the forest seem more dense.

First off, for trees that are further off in the distance, behind the existing trees, we can make very low-poly versions by rendering the side view of one of the full-res trees and using that as the texture. Take a look at Figure 10.22; I've rendered out the side view of one of our trees and saved it as a 32-bit targa with alpha.

10.21 A small grouping of the duplicated tree.

10.22 A rendered side view of the tree, saved with alpha.

Now I assign that new texture to two simple planes that intersect. This is typically called a cross-poly or billboard (see Figure 10.23).

You can see that when placed behind the higher poly trees, the four-poly trees are nearly indistinguishable from the rest, and we've saved *a lot* of polys this way (see Figure 10.24).

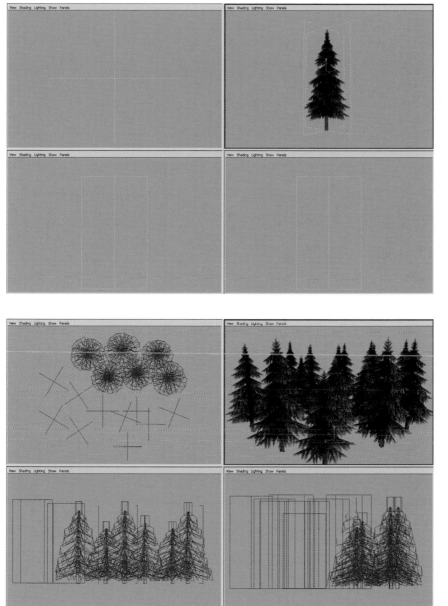

10.23 The rendered texture applied to two cross-polys to make a very low-poly version of the tree.

10.24 Using the low-poly version of the tree to fill in the background.

To take the idea even further, I've created a plane in the background and tiled the rendered texture across this long plane to add even more depth. Two or three of these offset from one another with their verts tweaked will give us even more density with even fewer polys (see Figure 10.25). By duplicating the outer plane and making some variations, you add even more depth to the scene (see Figure 10.26).

10.25 Using very simple planes with the same texture tiled across.

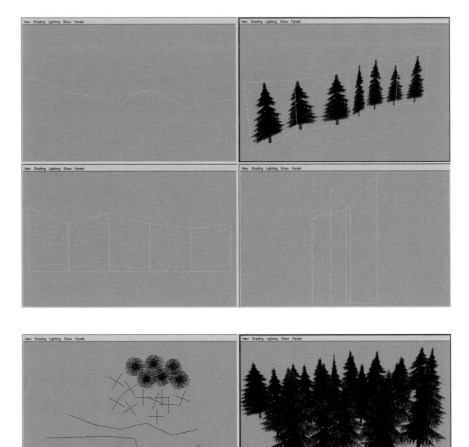

10.26 An even denser forest.

An entire forest with only three textures and a minimal amount of polys! This is just another example of how powerful alpha can be when modeling for games. Using the ideas presented here with the pine tree, you can create virtually any kind of vegetation from trees to bushes to vines.

REFLECTION

One thing that nearly all games lack is true reflection. The computing power needed to calculate accurate reflection is currently out of reach for games. So what do we do as artists in situations like this? We find a way to fake it.

Oftentimes we use reflection maps to create the illusion that an object is reflecting the environment around it by using a small texture. That works fine for a shiny sphere in a room, but what about standing water? I'm going to continue to use the pine tree as an example for the next lesson.

Let's say we have our pine trees sitting on the bank of a lake. Take a look at Figure 10.27.

A great trick for faking reflection is to simply mirror geometry in the Y axis (Z if you are working in 3ds max). If you study the reflections in the real world, you'll notice that's essentially what you are seeing—a mirror reflection of the objects. Here I selected all the trees and mirrored them (−1 in the vertical axis). Figure 10.28 shows how it creates the illusion of a perfect reflection.

Use this method for rivers, lakes, puddles, and so on. Of course, the drawback is that you are doubling your polys in most cases. Do keep in mind that the reflected geometry could be made up entirely of the four-poly cross trees and still have the same effect.

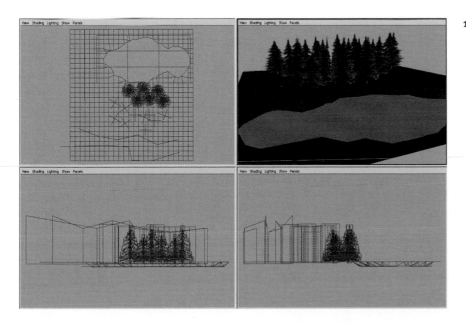

10.27 The grouping of trees, sitting on the bank of a lake.

10.28 Mirroring the geometry −1 in the vertical axis helps create the illusion of reflection in the water.

PLACED SHADOWS

Another trick I frequently use alpha for is creating mock shadows in a scene. As game technology advances, correct real-time shadows are becoming more and more common. Even with all the options of pixel shaders, lightmaps, and vertex lighting, you can probably count on situations where an artist will need to generate and place a shadow manually. Whether the shadow is for a pick-up item or a moving vehicle, knowing how to fake shadows in an inexpensive way is a valuable skill.

THE IMPORTANCE OF SHADOW

We tend to take shadow for granted. Look around the room and study various objects and their shadows. No matter the lighting conditions, every object has some sort of shadow that grounds it to the surface it's sitting on and makes it look as though it belongs in that space. No matter how subtle that shadow is, there is no question that the area around that object is affected by it. It's hard to imagine the objects around you without shadow, but if you look at the majority of games, you'll find missing shadows everywhere!

In a game environment, if an object does not have a shadow, it just doesn't look right. It looks out of place, or as if it is floating. Take a look at the example in Figure 10.29.

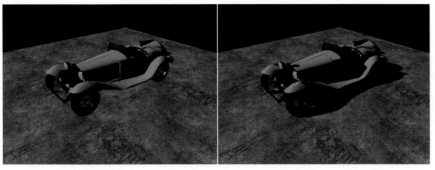

10.29 A car without and with a shadow.

Our brains know what to expect when we see something, and a shadow is an important detail. Objects without shadows stand out and just don't look like they belong in the scene. This is another one of my major pet peeves. Objects need to look like they are grounded and are part of the environment. We dream of the day when everything we place in our scene will receive and cast shadows perfectly. Until that day, if real-time shadows are not an option for your game, one option is to use alpha channels and place shadows manually underneath objects. It sounds like a lot of work and quite tedious, but it's actually more simple than you might think, and worth the extra time if you want a believable scene.

Whenever I create a new scene, I always make two specific textures, one called shadow_square.tga and another called shadow_circle.tga. You can find them on this book's web site. They typically look something like what is shown in Figure 10.30.

Using only these two versatile textures, you can create a mock shadow for almost any simple object. Let me explain.

Imagine we have a crate that is sitting on the ground. It has no shadow and looks out of place (see Figure 10.31). Now I'll create a two-poly plane and place it floating slightly above the ground below the box. By assigning shadow_square.tga to the plane, we get a mock shadow placed underneath the object. It ties the crate to the ground and makes it look like it actually belongs in the scene (see Figure 10.32).

10.30 Notice that the textures are solid black and rely solely on the alpha channel.

10.31 A crate without a shadow.

10.32 The simple two-poly plane with shadow_square.tga assigned.

Depending on the direction and angle of your light source, placing these fake shadows will rarely be technically accurate. Even so, you'll be surprised how much of a difference it makes.

Obviously, this works particularly well for scenes in which the light source is mostly above the object. But what if the light source is extreme and is hitting the object at a hard angle? Well, we do have options if we need the shadow to be more accurate. By going into component mode and selecting the vertices, you can move the verts to tweak the angle of the shadow (Figure 10.33).

An important point to remember about shadows is that the farther away the light source is from your object, the softer and more transparent the shadow will be. The closer it is, the more sharp, refined, and opaque the shadow will be. Imagine a movie theatre projector projecting images on a screen across the theatre. If you were to put your hand directly in front of the projector and make some hand animals, the shadow on the screen would be large and blurry. If you moved down in front of the screen and did the same thing, your hand's shadow would be clear and distinct. Figure 10.34 shows an example of this.

The distance of the light source from the object casting the shadow has a distinct effect on the shadow itself. Keep this in mind when you are placing mock shadows. By using the same texture, you can easily simulate these effects.

If you want the shadow edge to be more stark and sharp, simply scale the UVs outward, as shown in Figure 10.35.

10.33 By moving the vertices, you can manipulate the shadow to be more accurate for dramatic lighting situations.

10.34 How distance affects shadow.

10.35 Scaling the UVs outward to give the shadow a hard edge.

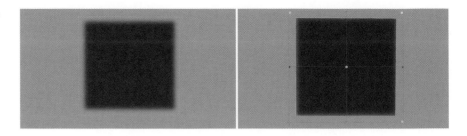

The other issue at hand is how to change the opacity of the shadow without creating another texture. Well, if you've done your reading, you already know the answer: vertex alpha (see Figure 10.36).

In the prior example, I reduced the opacity of the stretched outer vertices while keeping the verts closer to the box at their original opacity to accentuate the effect of the shadow fading with distance.

You can see that placing these fake shadows is quite flexible and very inexpensive. So what happens when we have objects that are circular? That is what the shadow_circle.tga texture is for. Use this texture for any object that is circular or oval. The same rules apply (see Figure 10.37).

All right, so we know this works great for square, rectangular, circular, or oval objects. What about something that is irregular in shape, like the unique table shown in Figure 10.38? By cutting polys or using the Split Polygon tool in Maya, you can subdivide the plane and tweak the verts until you have your desired shape.

10.36 Using vertex alpha to tweak the opacity of the shadow without creating a new texture.

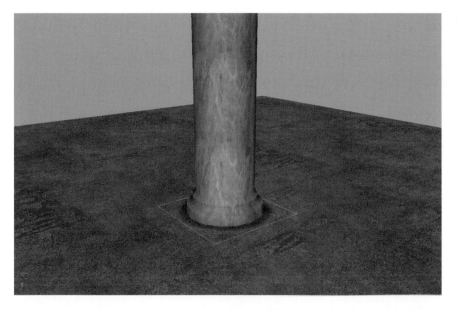

10.37 Using shadow_circle.tga to place a shadow underneath a cylindrical object.

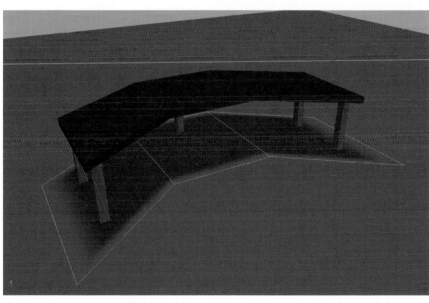

10.38 Using the same square texture, you can still get unique shapes.

When you are placing static shadows in your scene, the distance you lift them above the ground is important. Too high and it will be obvious the shadow is floating; too low and you will surely get Z-fighting. Z-fighting is a term used to describe the phenomenon of geometry seemingly "jumping" behind and in front of other objects.

I'm sure most of you have seen this occurring in games and even in the viewport of your 3D software package. When two polygons are too close together, they tend to fight over which one is displayed on top (see Figure 10.39).

This is an especially common issue with game engines. Even when you're working in max or Maya, you'll notice this happening in your viewport. The software gets confused as to which object should display first. In most game development environments, a programmer can help you by tagging each object to have a priority over another, but in most cases, just translating the objects a little farther way from one another will solve the problem.

It's remarkable how many objects you can provide shadows for using only square and circle textures. It would be ideal if you could get away with using them for the entire game, but some objects need more complexity in their shadows. Here is another little trick that can help give you more exact shadows for complex objects.

Let's go back to the pine tree again to further prove this point. A great way to make sure that your placed shadow is accurate to the object is to actually render out a top view of the object in 3D and save that render with an alpha channel. If I rendered out a top-down view of the tree and saved the image with alpha, I'd have something like what's shown in Figure 10.40. Now we can use this to make a shadow texture that will become part of the tree model (see Figure 10.41).

You can see how effective and inexpensive placing shadows manually in your scene can be. Even if your shadows don't match the light direction perfectly, they will still make a big difference in the realism of your scene. Just tying the objects to the ground will make them feel as if they belong in that space. So take the extra time when working to be sure that your objects have proper shadows, no matter how they are generated.

10.40 A top-down render of the tree.

10.41 Using the top-down render with alpha to make a shadow for the tree.

Conclusion

Hopefully, some the tips in this chapter have given you new ideas and ways to approach your art. Keep an open mind and remember that you often have to find unusual ways to achieve the visual results that you want to see. Just because it hasn't been done before doesn't mean it can't be done.

In the next chapter we'll talk about the user interface and heads-up displays.

CHAPTER 11

USER INTERFACE DESIGN AND CREATION

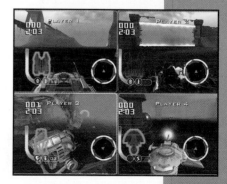

YOU COULD BE BUILDING THE greatest game in the world, but if it is not accessible and user-friendly, it will surely fail. That is why the user interface (UI) needs to be well thought-out and thoroughly tested during the development process. Although the decisions are typically a group effort among game designers, artists, and programmers, the visual composition and aesthetics play a key role in the development of a successful interface. Not only does the imagery and layout need to be solid and clean, but also as efficient and clear as possible for the player to understand. I'm sure many of you can think of a few games where you spent half an hour just trying to figure out how to get the game started. Bad interface design can quickly confuse and frustrate players. And that is not how you want to start the game experience. The job of a UI designer is one that requires not only a strong sense of design, but also the ability to think logically and understand the psychology of player/game interaction. In this chapter we'll discuss the common elements of game interfaces and take a look at what makes for a successful and user-friendly design.

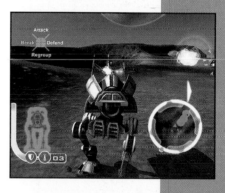

THE SHELL

The word *shell* describes the initial screens and menus a player encounters when first starting a game. The most basic purpose of a shell is to act as an introduction and a doorway to the gameplay. By offering options like Save and Load, controller configurations, and a good old Start button, you are allowing players to choose how and when they want to play the game.

More importantly, from an artistic standpoint, it's essential to remember that the shell is the first thing players will see when they play your game. It is the first opportunity to establish the tone, theme, and pacing while at the same time setting the player's expectations for the rest of the experience. Realizing that this opportunity exists and taking advantage of it is what makes for a truly good shell. It's very important that the visual style and feel of the shell is consistent with that of the game. For example, if the game is going to take place in a medieval/fantasy setting, the shell should not look high-tech and polished, but instead should look like something consistent with the medieval fantasy context.

Shells are as varied as games themselves. Some are extremely basic and require only a minimal amount of interaction, whereas others are complex and play more of a significant role in the overall game. The key is to understand the core focus of your game and create a shell that is representative of that focus.

For *Medal of Honor Frontline*™, we made the decision to give the shell a completely 3D look and feel, despite the fact that all the elements were simply 2D images rendered from 3D objects. Although creating a shell of this type is typically more challenging and complex than a traditional 2D interface, we felt it was extremely important to establish a strong sense of detail and immersion, which is the signature of the *Medal of Honor*™ series. By setting the stage up front, you prepare the player for the experience that lies ahead of them. Figure 11.1 shows the main screen from *Medal of Honor Frontline*™.

Breaking up any image into an arrangement of interactive elements that are consistent and reliable can present a difficult challenge. But taking the time to think everything through makes anything possible. A solid shell will bring the player into the game with a sense of excitement and eagerness. It is your job as an artist to produce and deliver the shell that will produce those feelings.

Basic adherence to information design principles ensures that an interface is clear, intuitive, and efficient. This can be done while also creating a unique visual style, and without resorting to clearly labeled buttons or tables of options; it just requires a lot of thought.

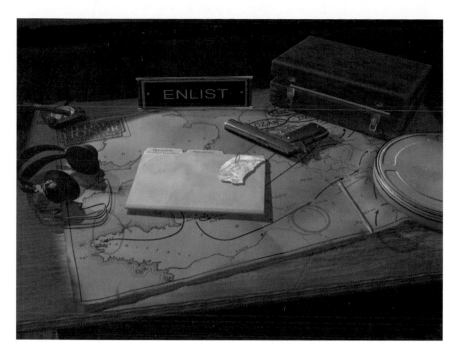

IN-GAME USER INTERFACE

Whether it's the pause screen, the options menu, or navigating a map, establishing a basic set of rules that the user can understand and identify with is the core goal of any interface. All the elements the user interacts with during his or her experience with the game are considered part of the UI. Whether it is a video game, a software package, or a web page, the end result has to be something logical and well thought out. Along with the need for intelligent and accessible interaction comes the responsibility of the artist to make something that is aesthetically pleasing.

Let's go back to the idea of establishing a basic set of rules. You don't want the user to have to relearn an interface every time a new screen appears. An interface works well when the important elements on the screen are predictable from one screen to the next. Setting rules allows you to do just that. If important text appears in the upper-left corner on one screen, any additional important text should appear in the same place. When you are playing a game, you shouldn't have to spend too much time trying to find information.

How you display that information is very important as well. Why are analog gauge speedometers and clocks easier to read than more accurate digital gauges? Because you don't have to read them: Your brain gets the desired information at a very low level. These same principles inform game UI as well: A health meter is more easily interpreted than a number of life points.

The level of sophistication and complexity of the game should be clearly reflected in the interface. Think about the target audience and their level of participation. Does the gameplay require only two buttons to play, like a jump button and a shoot button? Then your interface should stay simple and possibly use only those two buttons as well. Maybe your game is a complex massively multiplayer online role-playing game (MMORPG) like *Star Wars Galaxies* or *Everquest*. The level of complexity in that type of game calls for a more robust and complicated interface. But again, the target audience is accustomed to complex games and is less likely to be frustrated when dealing with multiple elements and commands. Figure 11.2 shows a great example of a successfully robust menu system from the turn-based role-playing game (RPG) *Gladius*.

Although the amount of information required for a game as complex as *Gladius* is significant, the UI designers made careful decisions about how to present the information. The screen is essentially divided into two major areas. You choose a gladiator on the left, and you are presented with the statistics on the right. Most of the text and information is focused on the right side of the screen. This holds true for most of the game, establishing a general rule.

11.2 A menu screen from *Gladius*.

HEADS-UP DISPLAY

The elements you see onscreen while playing a game are considered part of the heads-up display (HUD). In many games these elements are typically things like a health meter, map, or even the player's score. The trick with HUD design is to provide the player with the information necessary to play the game, without distracting from the gameplay itself. Your onscreen elements need to be clear and useful, yet subtle and unobtrusive; this presents a unique design challenge that has been dealt with in hundreds of creative ways over the years. Take a look at a few HUD designs from various games. Figure 11.3 shows a simple and effective use of space in *Star Wars: The Clone Wars* by LucasArts.

Star Wars: The Clone Wars has a simple and effective design, offering the player information on their health, ammo, and tactics, as well as a compass that provides info on direction and location of enemies.

HUDs become a more complex challenge when you are dealing with a multiplayer scenario. When your screen real estate is cut in half or more, the concept still has to work (see Figure 11.4).

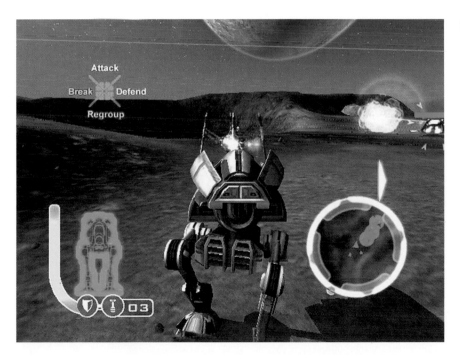

11.3 The HUD from *Star Wars: The Clone Wars.*

You want the most simple and clear interface possible, but more complex games often require more complex UIs to represent all of the possible choices and information the player needs to track (see Figure 11.5).

11.4 Multiplayer HUDs offer another challenge.

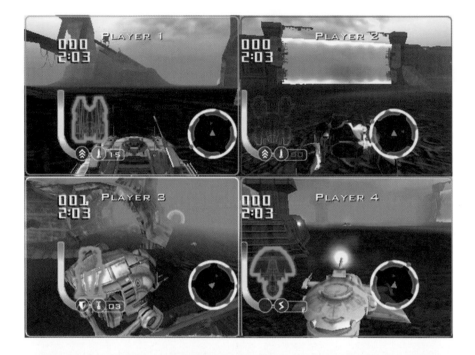

11.5 The more complex the gameplay, the more information you have to work with.

COMPOSITION

Think of composition as the assembly or construction of elements; it is an artistic arrangement that guides the viewer's eye and unifies the overall image.

I can't stress enough how important it is to make sure that your design adheres to a solid and intelligible composition. The purpose of a user interface is to bring the player into the game in the most clear and efficient way while providing an enjoyable and appealing experience. Having a comprehensible interface that is easy to understand and navigate takes the skilled eye of a designer. I strongly encourage you to study the foundations and principles of graphic design. Paying attention to positive and negative spaces, balance, color, and focus are essential to the process.

Let's start by talking about…you guessed it, broad strokes! All right, so you have a first-class plan, and everything sounds great in theory. Before you start to generate all the artwork, take some time to use basic placeholders to test your ideas and functionality. For the *Medal of Honor*™ shell, I started by blocking out the basic elements with simple geometry and worked with the programmer to implement and test our ideas. Figure 11.6 shows the blocked-out test.

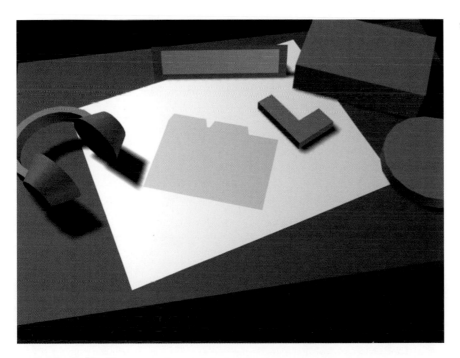

11.6 Use simple shapes to block out your UI.

Medal of Honor Frontline™ IMAGES COURTESY OF ELECTRONIC ARTS INC. © 2002 ELECTRONIC ARTS INC. ALL RIGHTS RESERVED.

PLAN, PLAN, PLAN

The most significant lesson to learn about interface design is to plan ahead. So many factors are involved in implementing a functional and user-friendly UI that you are bound to hit roadblocks along the way. The more you plan and experiment, the more smoothly the process will go. I'll do my best to address some of the more important considerations in the hopes that you can steer clear of the many possible pitfalls.

LOCALIZATION

Localization plays a very important part in interface design. When planning your design, you need to take many factors into consideration that are affected by the requirements of localizing your game. I'll discuss a few of them in the following sections.

NTSC AND PAL

When dealing with console games, one challenge you can count on is the conversion from NTSC to PAL. NTSC is the standard television video format (720×486) for countries like the United States, Canada, and the United Kingdom. Just like electrical outlets, other countries have a different standard and format for TV. PAL is the format used in dozens of countries from Germany and Spain to Portugal and Zanzibar. PAL resolution (720×576) is different enough from NTSC that it significantly changes the look of your design. The fact that text becomes stretched and parts of the screen can be cut off should be key considerations when planning. Many development teams build a pipeline early on that can automatically convert to PAL at any time. Smart move.

There are typically three ways to deal with NTSC to PAL conversion:

- Change the aspect ratio to a letterbox format.
- Crop the screen to fit the PAL aspect ratio.
- Change the dimensions of each individual image. (Tons of work and not worth the headache, but if you find yourself in a situation where you have to do it, *use Photshop's Actions!*)

SCREEN RESOLUTION

Even though NTSC and PAL are not considerations when making a PC game, there are similar challenges that need to be addressed. In the PC world, a HUD or graphical user interface (GUI) needs to adapt to wildly varying screen resolutions—anything from 800×600 to 1600×1200. Planning needs to take place to ensure that a GUI (especially the HUD) is readable and unobtrusive at lower resolutions but still legible at super-high resolutions.

TRANSLATION

In addition to PAL conversion, you need to take into account several other factors when designing your interface, not the least of which is character (text) length. One of the more intricate and time-consuming responsibilities is language translation. On the surface, it doesn't really sound all that difficult—just translate the words and switch them out, right? I wish it were that easy. You have to realize that in a situation where you are already being very careful with how much screen real estate you are taking up, a word in English translated into French or Italian is rarely going to have the same number of letters. Here is a good example. Say you have a command or a button in your interface that's called "Maximize." It fits nice and snug on your screen and looks great. But when it's to time to localize the German version of the game, you are going to discover that the German words for "Maximize" are "max-imieren Sie." Instead of 8 characters, you now have 13 and a space to deal with. One very helpful suggestion I can make is to use the hard-ware's capabilities for generating text. PlayStation 2, Xbox, and GameCube all have internal software for generating text on screen. Try to use the hardware capabilities to display text instead of typing all the text in Photoshop. It takes much less time to change text in code than to man-ually go into your PSD files and make changes for five languages.

Needless to say, it's a great idea to think things through as much as possi-ble in the early stages to avoid some very frustrating problems down the road. When planning your UI and interface, make sure everyone on the team understands what is required for localization. I've been in situations where the planning wasn't there, and I can guarantee that no matter how patient an artist you might be, you'll pull out your hair trying to make it all work in the end.

Again, the point is to think ahead and make a plan, realizing that you will have to make localized versions of your game, and that planning accordingly will make everyone happy.

HARDWARE APPROVAL

Along with the artistic standards required to produce a winning inter-face comes the strict regulations set by Sony, Microsoft, Nintendo, and other hardware manufacturers. There are stringent rules and conventions that need to be followed to get approval by these companies. Characters and text must be a certain size, title safe areas have to be observed, and rigid guidelines limit the artistic flexibility you would have in a more conventional design situation. It is extremely important to gather all the information from each of these manufacturers before you even begin to tackle the interface.

BUILDING THE UI

Creating an interface is not unlike creating a web page. As a matter of fact, many game UI artists that I know got their starts by designing and creating web pages. It shouldn't be surprising then that a lot of game developers use web creation software to build their UIs. Flash, Dreamweaver, and even FrontPage have been used to create some of the screens and menus you see in many of today's games.

The process of generating the assets for a UI can be a long and tedious one. It's not unusual for a typical screen to be composed of over 30–40 images—and that's just one screen. Organizing and managing your images and process is key. Agree on specific naming conventions with the programmers and use tools that make your workload manageable. One program I have found invaluable for UI creation is Adobe ImageReady. It is bundled with recent versions of Photoshop and is designed for creating web pages. Photoshop, with all its layers, filters, and actions, combined with the usability of a web creation program makes for an ideal user interface environment. ImageReady uses "slices" to divide large images into individual elements and allows for easy rollovers and button clicks.

CONCLUSION

Too often the UI takes a backseat to the rest of production and isn't addressed until the later stages of development. That is when problems tend to occur. Whether you are directly involved with the UI or not, talk to the team and be sure it is getting the attention it needs.

Up to this point, we've explored *with a broad stroke* a significant amount of information regarding creating game art. In the next chapter, we're going to take that information and talk about how to put it all together and add the finishing touches.

[CHAPTER] **12**

WRAPPING IT UP

SO WE'VE REACHED THE END, and everything is done, right?
WRONG! Sorry to disappoint you, but even at this late stage,
there is still a lot of work to be done. But, on the bright side, it's
still really fun work. I won't lie to you; in game development, this
is the time when you are going to be working insane hours, sleeping at the office, and eating more pizza than you could ever imagine. You'll be walking around in the same clothes for days at a time,
and wishing you could get caffeine intravenously. You've spent a
year or more working closely with your team, collaborating on
ideas, and coming up with solutions to some of the most difficult
of roadblocks, but now the whole team can see the final product
coming together. It's the light at the end of the tunnel, the home
stretch, the Holy Grail.

Well, we have covered quite a bit of information up to this point,
and whether you realize it or not, you now know many of the
ideas and techniques you'll need to set yourself apart as an exceptional game artist. Many of the terms, workflows, and technologies
will change over time, but the purpose of this book was to teach
you the foundational skills and practices that will give you the
opportunity to set new standards in the industry and generate work

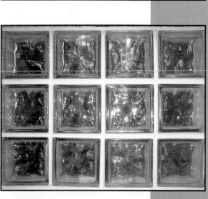

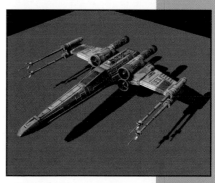

that is of the highest quality. To wrap things up, this chapter will focus on how to bring all the work and creativity together and put the finishing touches on what will be your game. We'll discuss the process of tidying up the art, fixing bugs, and adding some of the final pieces such as skydomes and collision geometry. We should start by talking about source control.

SOURCE CONTROL

As you work in a production environment, keeping track of resources and files becomes extremely important. Source control is a generic term for a very specific system of check-ins and check-outs in a database. You'll have to familiarize yourself with whatever source control software your company uses and learn the concept of checking out and checking in your files. The idea is simple: Source control is meant not only to be a safeguard against losing data or breaking the game, but also to keep asset versions and to prevent others from simultaneously modifying assets.

Why mess with checking out a file? Let's say you have a tree in your level that you want to work on. By checking the file out, you are essentially temporarily taking it out of the game to make changes. With source control software, anyone on the team can look at the database and see that you have that tree checked out.

OK, so you work on the tree, add some polys, fix the texture, and now you want to check the file back *in* to the game.

Imagine, for example, that the tree in your level originally had 120 polygons, and it fit perfectly into your polygon budget. When you checked it out, you added another 50 polys and increased the resolution of the texture. If you check the tree back in and it exceeds your current budget, it could theoretically break or crash the game. Of course this is a very exaggerated example, but I think you get the idea. The point is to protect the game and ensure its stability by testing the changes yourself before you check the files back in. You can count on spending a lot of time using source control in the latter stages of development. Being careful with your check-ins and check-outs leads to a continually more solid game.

Now that you understand the concept of source control, let's talk about collision geometry.

COLLISION GEOMETRY

Contrary to what you may think, there are typically two sets of geometry in every game. There is the art, which you of course created and perfected and are very proud of, but we can't forget the invisible and underestimated collision geometry. As the player moves through your scene, how does the engine know what is a wall? What is a floor? What is a window? When the character is walking down a hallway, what happens when it bumps into a wall? It's stopped, right? Well, that's not the actual art the character is running into; it's collision geometry.

Collision geometry is a simplified, nontextured, and invisible version of the art that determines where the player can walk and what types of surfaces the player is encountering. The art geometry and the collision geometry are normally separated because collision geometry does not need to be as detailed as the art. Now, even though collision is invisible, it still works against your poly count. In fact, if your collision geometry was identical to your art, not only would the poly count be doubled, but the player would always be bouncing off objects or getting stuck or hung up due to the excessive detail. The gameplay would be erratic and rough. Collision is typically very simple, flat, and basic. It doesn't need small details like textures or extra subdivisions because it is not being lit.

There is also no need to have collision geometry for art that the player will never bump into, like distant trees or buildings. It really only needs to serve as a guide for the characters to tell them where they can and cannot go. In more recent games, programmers have found effective ways to generate collision geometry automatically from the art. Trust me, this is a huge time saver. Manually creating collision geometry can be very time-consuming and frustrating. But don't rely solely on the programmers, because you'll most likely have to create some collision polys at some point. Let's take a look at a couple of examples. Figure 12.1 shows a starfighter from *Star Wars* and its simple collision geometry.

For environments where you have walls, floors, props, and the like, the idea is the same. Take a look at the room shown in Figure 12.2 from the polygon reduction exercise. By using the most simple shapes, you can quickly lay out effective collision geometry. Notice that we don't need any subdivisions on the walls or floor as long as they are flat.

For organic terrain where you have peaks and valleys, the collision geometry will need to be more accurate to ensure that the characters look as though they are walking on the ground properly and not sinking or floating.

12.1 Keep the geometry as simple as possible while being true to the form of the model.

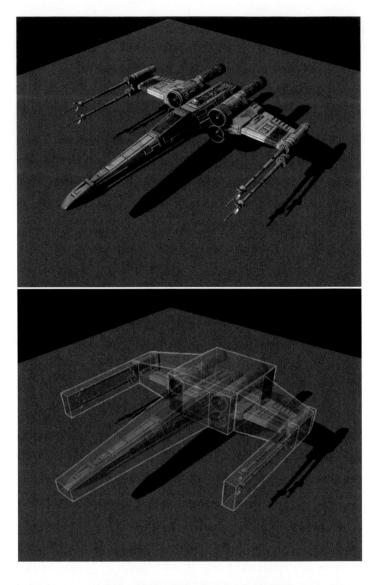

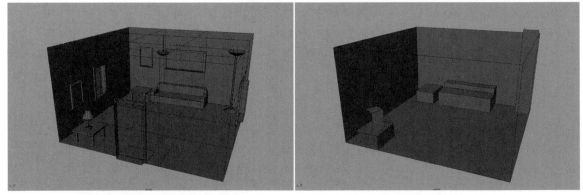

12.2 Simple collision geometry for the room.

SKYDOMES

Depending on the type of game you are making, you may or may not be responsible for creating a skydome. A skydome doesn't necessarily have to be a dome; you'll often hear it referred to as a skybox as well. The skydome is just like it sounds, typically a large dome or box with a sky texture applied to it that encompasses your scene to create the illusion that your environment is in the real world.

Let's look at how to create a skydome. I typically remove the bottom half of a simple sphere (see Figure 12.3). Because the dome is far away, it doesn't need to be too complex.

Next, flip the normals. This does two things. Because the game is taking place inside the sphere, flipping the normals allows you to texture and render the inside of the sphere rather than the default outer surface. Flipping the normals also allows you to see through the dome when working on the scene in 3D (see Figure 12.4).

Now, let's assign a texture. Obviously, the more detailed your sky needs to be, the higher resolution the map will need to be. Let's use a 512×512 texture and make sure it will tile on the sides (see Figure 12.5).

Notice the range of hills at the bottom of the texture; these can help make the world feel more expansive and can be used to establish a sense of scale. You'll also notice that the top part of the image is more uniform in color. This is done to prevent some mapping and pinching issues that typically occur with spherical mapping.

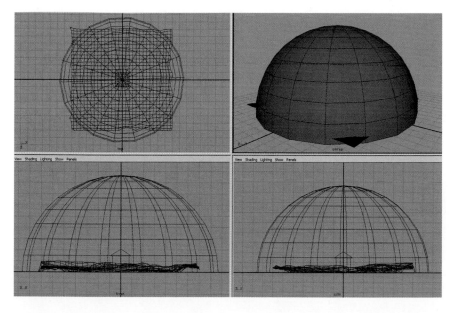

12.3 Using half of a sphere for the skydome geometry.

12.4 Flipping the normals to see inside while working.

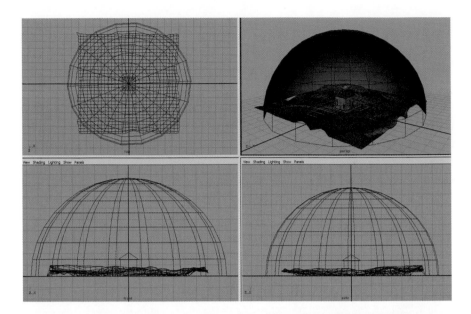

12.5 The tilable skydome texture.

With the texture assigned, a cylindrical projection will work well. Now if we move the camera inside the dome, you can see the sky we have created (see Figure 12.6).

I want to mention a few tricks you can use with skydomes. An easy way to have moving clouds in the distance is to have two skydomes, one slightly smaller than the other. The outer dome has your sky texture and sun or moon. The inner dome has just alpha clouds. If the programmers can get the inner dome to rotate slowly, you'll have great-looking moving clouds in your scene (see Figure 12.7).

At the same time you are working on collision geometry or skydomes, you may be responsible for creating light volumes as well.

12.6 The skydome.

12.7 The two skydome textures; the cloud texture has a soft alpha channel.

LIGHT VOLUMES

Although building light volumes is not as necessary in most of today's more advanced games, I think it's important to talk about the functionality. Light volumes, like collision geometry, are invisible boxes or spheres. However, these boxes or spheres are associated with lights in certain areas. The purpose of light volumes is to create conditions such that when characters enter a room that is lit completely red, they too will have red light cast on them. Remember that when you are using vertex lighting, there are no actual 3D lights in the scene, just lighting on a per-vertex basis. So it would look funny if a character walks into a red room and is not lit red as well. A lighting volume defines an area and lets the engine know what type of lighting information to cast on the character, while ignoring the vertex lighting in the scene. As you know, there are several ways to light the scene in a game, and with many of today's more advanced engines, you can actually place 3D light in the scene to light the art geometry. The lighting information is carried from the 3D software into the game engine and used to light the characters as well.

TAGGING MATERIALS

Tagging materials or geometry is an important responsibility of the artist for many games. Although it really depends on the type of game you are making, the concept is quite simple. For each material or texture in the game, the artist assigns different traits. The purpose is to further define what the surfaces are and how they react in the game world. For example, in Figure 12.8 you would tag the texture as Wood_Medium, which would tell the engine the following things about the texture:

- When a bullet hits the texture, it will emit a medium-colored wood particle, leave a medium-colored wood bullet decal, and make a wood bullet impact sound.

- When a character walks across the texture, the footsteps will sound like they are on wood.

Surfaces can also be tagged with characteristics like glow, animate (cycle through several frames), or pass through (meaning bullets or characters can pass through the texture).

12.8 For a wood texture like this, you can tag several properties.

Tagging can be done in many different ways. It can be as simple as a specific naming convention that you and the team agree on; for example, you may save out the wood texture as Wood_1_WM, with WM meaning Wood_Medium. Although tagging by naming convention is effective, you can get more control and flexibility if you have a system set up in your 3D software that lets you choose more specific options on a per-material basis by using drop-down boxes or check boxes to assign characteristics. Imagine you have a glass block window texture, as shown in Figure 12.9.

This is a good example of a situation where you might need a bit more control over the tagging. Unlike normal glass, which a bullet will pass through and cause a glass particle to be emitted, a glass shattering sound, and probably a swap of the texture for a broken version, glass block needs a different set of rules. It should not allow bullets to pass through; it shouldn't emit a glass particle, but just small glass chips; it should leave a decal; and the sound should be more subdued and not a shatter. Having the ability to choose very specific characteristics on a per-material basis is the safest bet if it is important that your game's world be interactive and realistic. Tagging is done in many ways, sometimes within the 3D application by an artist, and other times in code by programmers.

12.9 A glass block window texture may need characteristics that are unique to this type of glass.

BUG FIXING

Next comes the wonderful world of bug fixing. Think your geometry and collision were perfect? Think again. I will admit that the artist typically has fewer bugs to deal with than the programmers (who, in part, have more bugs to dispatch because of something we as artists did), but your list of bugs can seem overwhelming.

By this time, you could personally have hundreds of bugs that are assigned to you. This means you are fully responsible for fixing them. (We'll discuss some examples in the following sections.) To reach Alpha, many teams insist that there be no "A" bugs in the database. The term differs from company to company, but usually "A" bugs are the ones that crash or break the game and are considered the most serious. Depending on the classification system, you might encounter a system consisting of A, B, C, and D bugs, along with priority numbers associated with them. For example, the most serious bugs would be A-1. The least serious (like a slightly blurry texture off in the distance that most players will never notice) would be a D-4 bug.

Let me list some of the most common bugs you can expect to have to deal with as an artist. Bug fixing is the truest test of your problem-solving skills and patience. If you can survive it, you'll be a better artist for it.

COLLISION ISSUES

The player gets stuck in a room, can't jump in areas, walks through walls, or even falls through the floor and disappears forever. You'll find that the majority of your "vertex surgery" (welding and cleaning up) will take place in the latter stages of development as you are assigned bugs. Even one unwelded vert can cause a player to get stuck or fall through the collision geometry. Whether collision is generated from the art itself or built by hand, you can count on some really interesting and frustrating scenarios that you'll have to troubleshoot and deal with yourself.

Z-FIGHTING AND PROBLEM NORMALS

Many common art bugs have to do with faces that are either reversed, missing, or Z-fighting with other faces. You can expect to spend some time going through your scene with a fine-toothed comb, flipping normals, welding verts and edges, and moving faces apart.

The same issues can also cause small seams and slivers in the geometry that not only look bad, but also can potentially mess up collision and gameplay.

JUST PLAIN UGLY ART

No matter how good of an artist you are, you are still capable of making ugly art. Sometimes you are in a hurry, or just don't notice something until the end. But as the pieces of your scene come together, objects and environments won't always look perfect together. Rely on critique from other artists and testers to point out blemishes that you may have missed.

Along with the scenarios listed here, you can count on many different bugs of varying types to be put on your plate. Nearly everything we've discussed in this book can be a potential bug. Experience and patience will go a long way in avoiding and fixing bugs. Reducing the number of bugs allows you more time to put the final artistic touches on your work.

POLISHING

There is obviously a good deal of work to do during the final stages of development. At the same time you are fixing bugs, tagging materials, and tweaking collision geometry, you should also be taking the opportunity to really polish and perfect your overall work. At this point, you should be able to sit down in front of a TV and play through the game, looking closely at each mission or level, making sure that everything works well together and looks great. You should have the chance to do overall color adjustments on a per-level basis, possibly making a night scene slightly lighter or darker, or maybe desaturating a distractingly colorful level. Having the time and the standards to make one last pass over the game will make for a stronger piece of work.

The bottom line here is that throughout this book, we've made a point to continually set new goals and standards for ourselves. Consistently and continually improving as artists is the most important lesson to be learned. As long as you are taking your work to the next level and thinking about the fundamentals of art, you'll surely set yourself apart as an exceptional artist. In order to provide clearly defined goals for the final stages of development and to plan and track progress, you need some structure. That is what milestones are for.

MAJOR MILESTONES

This is without question the most strenuous and potentially stressful time of development. The last few months of production typically show the most incredible leaps and bounds as the elements of the game come together. Before you know it, you'll actually be playing your game, new features and artwork will appear daily, and the entire package will be coming into view. Because so many parts of the game are quickly being thrown into the mix, it's important to set up a standard set of rules and guidelines to ensure that you are on track and continually improving. The most important milestones in development are typically Alpha and Beta.

ALPHA

Alpha, the first stage of completion, is typically defined differently by each company, team, and project, but the idea is usually the same: to establish a clear set of goals that prove everything works the way it's supposed to. This is often referred to as proof of concept. It is making sure that all your ideas are in place and functional while nailing down the scope of your game. After Alpha is achieved, the idea is that nothing really changes; the rest of the time is spent tweaking and fixing. You might also hear Alpha referred to as content complete, meaning that everything that will be in the game is in the game, and working. Again, the exact definition of Alpha changes from game to game, but there are a few goals you can count on as requirements from an artist.

FINAL ART

At this point there is no more stand-in or temporary art. Everything that you see in the game should be final. (I know it sounds harsh, but don't be afraid; there is usually room for small changes all the way up until Beta, as long as they don't break the game.) For example, if you had a simple box in place of a car that will eventually be there, it's time to take that out and replace it with the real thing to be sure that it doesn't cause a bug.

FULLY FUNCTIONAL USER INTERFACE

The user interface (UI) should be completely functional, and no more changes should be made to the design. Trust me, you don't want any changes to the UI at this point in the game! This is another reason to be sure that the UI gets the team's full attention early in production.

BUGS

A common requirement of Alpha is to eliminate all "A" bugs, or bugs that are the most severe. Any bug that crashes the game in any way should be considered an "A" bug and have priority over any other bug. Thankfully, bugs that are this damaging are not normally due to art; more often than not, they tend to be a programming issue.

BETA

The Beta milestone, like Alpha, can be defined differently depending on the project, but Beta is typically meant to be the first final version of the game. The goal of Beta is to have *zero* bugs. The game should essentially be finished. Additional bugs can and will most likely appear after Beta as you deal with localization and additional testing, but the idea is clear: a fully functional game that is content complete, fully playable, and bug-free. Your responsibilities as an artist at this stage in the game are theoretically minimal.

As we talked about in the last chapter, localization can be a time-consuming and difficult task if you have not planned properly. During Beta, it's likely you'll be responsible for making subtle changes to art due to language or cultural differences. Maybe it's removing an image that may be offensive in other countries, or replacing words with their proper translations.

In addition to localization issues, I have found that collision bugs still find a way to pop up even at this late stage. By now, the collision bugs should be cosmetic or subtle. By Beta, the player or characters should never get stuck or fall through the world.

Once you and your team can declare Beta, you are one step closer to a final game.

GOLD

All done! Gold is everyone's favorite milestone. Off the production line and ready for the shelf. The word *Gold* conjures up images of vacation time and refocus. Once the game is complete and has been approved by all the hardware manufacturers, you can pat yourself on the back and celebrate the impending success of your game. It's not uncommon for a game to go Gold within weeks of its release date. Of course, we'd all prefer not to cut it so close, but sometimes that is what has to be done. But just like anything else, you want to have the best product possible by the time it becomes available to the public, so working down to the wire is more common than you might think.

On that note, I'd like to say that this book has officially gone Gold.

Conclusion

I've had a fantastic time putting this all together and hope that the information in this book has proven to be valuable. I'm very excited about and proud of the game industry and look forward to seeing where it will lead us in the future. My hopes are that by passing on the knowledge that I have gained over the years, I can help expedite and improve the creative process and visual fidelity of games in the long term. I'm counting on you as an artist to continue improving on and setting new standards by empowering the creativity within you and embracing the challenges that lie ahead of you.

INDEX

Visit Peachpit on the Web at www.peachpit.com

- Read the latest articles and download timesaving tipsheets from best-selling authors such as Scott Kelby, Robin Williams, Lynda Weinman, Ted Landau, and more!

- Join the Peachpit Club and save 25% off all your online purchases at peachpit.com every time you shop—plus enjoy free UPS ground shipping within the United States.

- Search through our entire collection of new and upcoming titles by author, ISBN, title, or topic. There's no easier way to find just the book you need.

- Sign up for newsletters offering special Peachpit savings and new book announcements so you're always the first to know about our newest books and killer deals.

- Did you know that Peachpit also publishes books by Apple, New Riders, Adobe Press, Macromedia Press, palmOne Press, and TechTV press? Swing by the Peachpit family section of the site and learn about all our partners and series.

- Got a great idea for a book? Check out our About section to find out how to submit a proposal. You could write our next best-seller!

You'll find all this and more at www.peachpit.com. Stop by and take a look today!

VOICES THAT MATTER

VISIT OUR WEB SITE

WWW.NEWRIDERS.COM

On our Web site you'll find information about our other books, authors, tables of contents, indexes, and book errata. You will also find information about book registration and how to purchase our books.

EMAIL US

Contact us at this address: **nrfeedback@newriders.com**

- If you have comments or questions about this book
- To report errors that you have found in this book
- If you have a book proposal to submit or are interested in writing for New Riders
- If you would like to have an author kit sent to you
- If you are an expert in a computer topic or technology and are interested in being a technical editor who reviews manuscripts for technical accuracy

- To find a distributor in your area, please contact our international department at this address. **nrmedia@newriders.com**

- For instructors from educational institutions who want to preview New Riders books for class-room use. Email should include your name, title, school, department, address, phone number, office days/hours, text in use, and enrollment, along with your request for desk/examination copies and/or additional information.
- For members of the media who are interested in reviewing copies of New Riders books. Send your name, mailing address, and email address, along with the name of the publication or Web site you work for.

BULK PURCHASES/CORPORATE SALES

The publisher offers discounts on this book when ordered in quantity for bulk purchases and special sales. For sales within the U.S., please contact: Corporate and Government Sales (800) 382-3419 or **corpsales@pearsontechgroup.com**.
Outside of the U.S., please contact: International Sales (317) 428-3341 or **international@pearsontechgroup.com**.

WRITE TO US

New Riders
1249 Eighth Street
Berkeley, California 94710

CALL US

Toll-free (800) 571-5840. Ask for New Riders.
If outside U.S. (317) 428-3000. Ask for New Riders.

New
Riders

Maximize Your Impact

As THE game resource, NRG books explore programming, design, art, and celebrity savvy. NRG takes you behind the scenes... revealing insider secrets like never before.

0735714096
Matthew Omernick
US$39.99

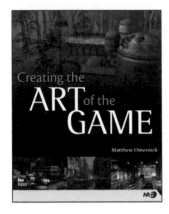

0321278909
Chris Crawford
US$34.99

1592730078
David Freeman
Foreword by Will Wright
US$49.99

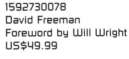

073571438X
Antony Ward
US$49.99

0735714134
Alexander Brandon
US$34.99

New Riders